READER'S DIGEST

Fast & Fabulous

Low-Sew
Bathroom Projects

READER'S DIGEST

Fast & Fabulous

Low-Sew
Bathroom Projects

By the editors of *Handcraft Illustrated* magazine

The Reader's Digest Association, Inc.
Pleasantville, New York/Montreal

A Reader's Digest Book

Conceived and edited by the Editors of *Handcraft Illustrated*
Designed by Amy Klee

Library of Congress Cataloging in Publication Data
Low-sew bathroom projects / by the editors of Handcraft illustrated.
      p.   cm. — (Reader's Digest fast and fabulous)
  ISBN 0-7621-0091-5
  1. Household linens. 2. House furnishings. 3. Bathrooms.
  I. Handcraft illustrated. II. Series: Fast and fabulous.
TT387.L695   1998   98-5472
646.2'1—dc21

Printed in the United States of America

Introduction

In many ways, the bathroom is a perfect place for make-at-home sewing projects. For most of us, the space is relatively small, meaning the projects in turn are small scale. If you need to purchase fabric, in most cases the required yardage is small, and can be matched easily by taking a small swatch of paint or wallpaper to the store with you. This book is a collection of beautiful and functional sewing projects that you can make and use in your bathroom, or give as gifts.

Chapter One, Tub and Shower, features several projects designed for use in and around the bathtub. Organize your shower soap, razor, and washcloth in the mesh Shower Hammock. When you step out of the bath, place your feet on a knit Shag Rug, or a piqué mat embellished with letters sewn from grosgrain ribbon.

In Chapter Two, Vanity, you'll find a variety of small touches that can bring a sense of elegance and coziness to your dressing room. Stitch up a Drawstring Makeup Pouch, made from two circles of fabric with a drawstring threaded in between, for a beautiful addition to your vanity countertop or shelf. Or quick - sew a padded footstool using white piqué.

Looking for added extras that move a bath from purely functional to simply elegant? The projects in Chapter Three can help.

For special occasions, line your towel rack with Accented Guest Towels or the Lace-Inset Hand Towels. Fill your drawers with Quick Silk Sachets, and store your perfume and bath sundries in a Fabric-Covered Tray. Last but not least, you can even dress up an ordinary wastebasket with a fabric liner.

Decorating your shower and windows has never been easier. Chapter Four features such projects as a pull shade, which can be custom-fit to any window, and a picket-style window valance that will add a cheerful top edging to any plain window. The photo transfer shower curtain, on the other hand, is designed to brighten up the exterior of your shower.

This book will provide you with everything you need for producing bath decorations that you are proud of. The full-color photographs, step-by-step directions, and hand-drawn illustrations are designed to support you every step of the way. And, if you are so inspired, you can adapt each project's materials and style to suit your own taste and make each project uniquely your own.

Carol Endler Sterbenz
Editor, Handcraft Illustrated

Contents

Tub and Shower

Vanity

Windows and Walls

Shelf and Counter

Appendix

tub and shower

Herbal Bath Bolster

Who can resist creating comfort and a sense of relaxation at the same time? You can easily achieve both with this beautiful bath bolster. The outer case of the bolster, made from a dinner napkin, covers an inner pillow form, which is made of rolled batting sprinkled with dried herbs such as lavender, peppermint, chamomile, or lemon balm. The pillow protects your head from the edge of the tub and the steam rising from the water will release the scent of the herbs.

—

When purchasing batting for this project, select a completely synthetic batting that will dry quickly when it is splashed with bath water.

MATERIALS

- 1.5oz (50g) dried herbs
- 23in (57.5cm) square dinner napkin
- 1⅝yd (1.5m) 2in (5cm)-wide white eyelet trim
- 40in (1m) ⁵⁄₁₆in (.8cm)-diameter white cord
- ⅝yd (57cm) 45in (112.5cm)-wide muslin
- Crib-size (45 x 60in [112.5 x 150cm]) soft synthetic batting
- White sewing thread
- 54in (135cm) cotton string
- 2 rubber bands or hair elastics
- Fray preventer

YOU'LL ALSO NEED

Sewing machine; iron; sewing shears; rotary cutter; straight pins; large safety pin; narrow ribbon in matching or contrasting color.

Instructions:

1. Sew bolster case with eyelet trim. Fold napkin in half, wrong side out, and stitch edge opposite fold in a ½in seam (see illustration A, facing page). Press seam open. Cut eyelet trim in half crosswise. At each end of tube, pin trim so decorative edge is even with edge of napkin and right sides are together. Fold and

overlap one cut end to conceal raw edges. Stitch almost 2in (5cm) from edge all around. Turn tube right side out (illustration B).

2. Sew muslin cover for bolster form. Using rotary cutter or shears, cut 21 x 24½in (52.5 x 62cm) rectangle from muslin. Fold rectangle in half crosswise and stitch ½in (1.2cm) seam on 21in (52.5cm) edge opposite fold. Press seam to one side. Narrow hem, then fold and press each end 1in (2.5cm) to inside. Stitch ¾in (1.8cm) from each fold all around to form casing at each end. To make opening in casings, cut 1in (2.5cm) opening, then fold raw edges under and press. Cut string in half and use large safety pin to draw 27in (67.5cm) length of string through each casing. Tie string ends together (illustration C).

3. Make rolled bolster form. Unfold packaged batting into 30 x 45in (75 x 112.5cm) rectangle (double thickness), then cut two 13 x 45in (32.5 x 112.5cm) strips. Sprinkle herbs evenly over surface of both pieces. Starting at short edge, roll one batting strip into log about 4in (10cm) in diameter, then butt in second strip and continue rolling until diameter measures 7in (18cm) (illustration D). Insert log into muslin cover, pull drawstrings closed and tie off each end. Tuck loose strings inside bolster form, then insert into bolster case (illustration E).

4. Finish bolster. Gather fabric at each end of bolster and secure with rubber band. Cut cord in half, knot ends to prevent raveling, and tie around gathered bolster ends (illustration F). Seal cord ends with fray preventer and let dry.

Making the Herbal Bath Bolster

A. Sew two edges of a square napkin together to make a tubular case.

B. Turn the case right side out and line each inside edge with eyelet trim.

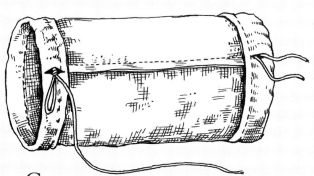

C. Sew a drawstring casing from muslin for the bolster form.

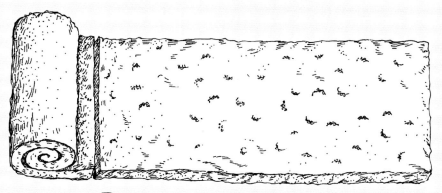

D. Sprinkle dried lavender or other herbs across the batting, then roll it up.

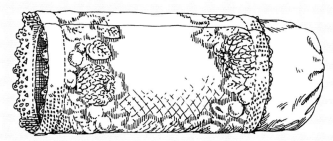

E. Place the roll inside the muslin cover, then insert the form into the case.

F. Gather the fabric at both ends, then tie the ends with white cord.

Striped Floor Runner

Looking for a quick and easy way to update your bathroom rug? You can custom-design a striped mat by cutting and stitching together pieces of several inexpensive bath mats. The new runner will match your decor and fit your space requirements exactly. This runner requires two or more single-color bath mats with rubbery nonskid backings. Each mat is cut crosswise into strips, then reassembled by butting the cut edges together and stitching with carpet thread. Because all the strips are cut crosswise, the bound edges of the mats become the bound edges of the runner, eliminating the need for any further finishing.

———

If you have a large amount of rug scraps left over from this project, stitch them together and make a smaller mat for in front of the sink or toilet.

MATERIALS

Yields one runner up to 60in (150cm) long

■ **Two or three contrasting 17 x 24in (42.5 x 61cm) bath mats**

■ **Neutral carpet thread**

YOU'LL ALSO NEED:

large quilter's acrylic grid ruler; pencil; graph paper; sharp scissors; and embroidery needle.

Instructions

1. Draft design. Determine required length for runner (e.g., 17in wide x 42in long [42.5cm wide x 105cm long]). Draft rectangle to scale on graph paper. Select stripe design for mat (e.g., even stripes, thick-and-thin stripes, or random stripes), and add to your diagram. Indicate stripe colors, and number of stripes from left to right (see illustration A, next page). Tally widths of same color stripes to determine how many 24in (60cm)-long mats are needed.

2. Mark and cut mats. Select mat that matches color of stripe #1; turn face down. Measuring from short edge, mark width of stripe #1 and draft line parallel to edge. Label as section #1. Measure, mark, and label additional stripes of this color on same mat. Repeat process on remaining mat(s) to mark all numbered stripes. Note that curved corners cannot be used for interior stripes and must be cut away as waste (illustration B).

3. Cut and rejoin mats. Using scissors, cut on each line through rubbery backing; guide scissor blades between yarns whenever possible. Discard waste. Lay segments flat, wrong side up, in numbered order. Thread embroidery needle with 18in (45cm) strand upholstery thread. To join two segments, butt cut edges (do not overlap them) and whip together (illustration C). Repeat process to join all segments. Turn runner right side up. Rub each seam lightly to shed loose tufts of yarn and disguise join (illustration D).

Making the Striped Floor Runner

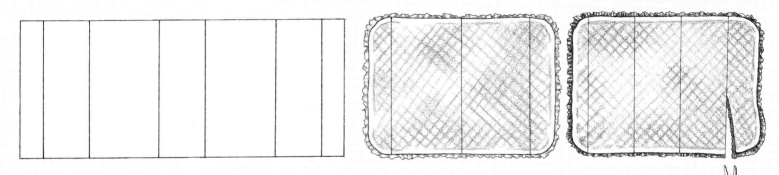

A. Draft the runner design to scale on graph paper.

B. Mark the stripes for each color on the mat backing.

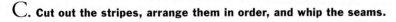

C. Cut out the stripes, arrange them in order, and whip the seams.

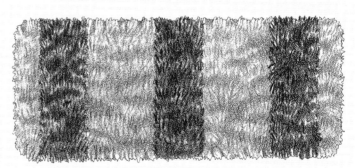

D. On the right side, fluff the yarn at each join.

Shower Hammock

Sponges, soaps, and loofahs can clutter up the rim of a bathtub, or litter the sinks and shelves of your bathroom. You can organize your bathroom accessories in one place, however, with this hammock-style holder, designed to hang from a shower curtain rod or the shower head. This project requires three primary materials: a thin metal ring, found with lampshade-making supplies, a string shopping bag, available in produce markets, and washable twill tape or cord. You can alter the length of your hammock according to what it will hold. Longer hammocks are well suited for loofahs and bath brushes, while shorter ones can hold sponges and soaps.

—

String bags and twill tape can be found in bright colors such as red, green, yellow, and black, or you can dye your bag and tape using fiber-reactive dye.

MATERIALS

- **String bag**
- **⅛in (3mm) metal lampshade ring measuring 8in (20cm) in diameter**
- **1yd (90cm) 1½in (4cm)-wide washable twill webbing**
- **1¼yd (115cm) ½in (1.2cm)-wide washable tape or cord (for hanging hammock)**

YOU'LL ALSO NEED

Sewing machine; sewing shears; matching thread; straight pins; and colorless nail polish to seal metal ring; optional: tissue paper strips.

SEWING TIP

Place paper over netting when machine sewing to prevent foot attachment "toes" from catching in the netting. The paper tears away easily after stitching.

Instructions:

1. Prepare metal ring. To prevent ring from rusting, paint with three coats nail polish, and let dry.

2. Establish size of hammock. Pin string bag over wire ring to determine desired size, tucking bag handles and edges to inner side of ring. Cut off handle and excess string bag. Hand-baste in place (see illustration A, facing page).

3. Sew hammock to ring. Using matching thread, machine stitch string bag in place over ring. Wire ring is thin enough to go under machine easily, so there is no need to remove foot. Remove hand-basted stitches.

4. Attach hangers. Divide narrow tape (or cord) into two pieces. If using cord, knot ends to prevent raveling. Pin ends of tape or cord at quarter intervals round outer side of ring, with cut ends facing up, and tape or cords crossing under hammock (illustration B).

5. Attach binding tape. Pin twill tape around outside top of hammock, covering first stitches and catching ends of tape or knots of cord. Fold short, raw end of webbing inwards ¼in (6mm) so that it forms a clean finish. Overlap turning by at least ¼in (6mm) at other end. Place pins crosswise so you can stitch slowly up to them, then remove them as you come to each one. Stitch twill in place below wire using ¼in (6mm) seams (illustration C).

6. Finish binding tape. Turn binding tape over to inner side of ring (illustration D). Leave at least ½in (1.2cm) on outer side. Pin binding, then stitch in groove between tape and string bag from outer side, catching edge of binding on inner side of ring in stitches (illustration E).

7. Finish hammock. Bring hanging tapes or cords up to cross above hammock. Catch both loops in hook and hang (illustration F).

Making the Shower Hammock

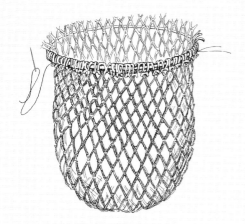

A. Hand-baste the string bag to a narrow metal ring.

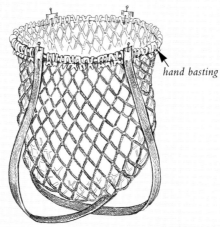

hand basting

B. Cut the tape into two pieces and pin in place on the outside of the ring, crossing under the hammock.

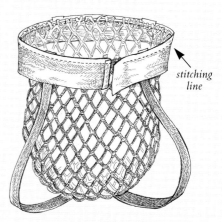

stitching line

C. Stitch the twill tape on the outside of the hanging tapes. Turn in the raw edges and overlap the ends.

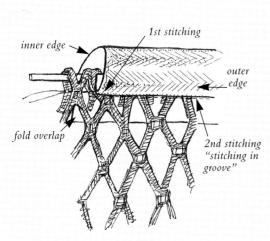

inner edge

1st stitching

outer edge

fold overlap

2nd stitching "stitching in groove"

D. Fold the twill tape over to the inner side, then overlap turning by ¼in (6mm).

E. Stitch in the groove between the tape and the string bag.

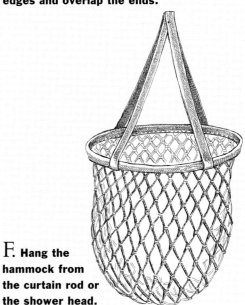

F. Hang the hammock from the curtain rod or the shower head.

23

Shag Bath Rug

If you can cast on, knit, and bind off, you can make this rag rug for your bathroom. The rug is made by knitting a web, into which strips of cut knit fabric are trapped. The first part of this project, cutting the strips of fabric, goes quickly if you use a rotary cutter. Before cutting the shag strips, cut a test strip across the fabric's grain and another one lengthwise, then examine them for curling and decide which orientation you prefer. Cutting across the grain produces flat strips, while cutting along it produces curled ones. To knit the first row of the rug, and the odd-numbered rows, use standard knitting. For the alternating shag rows, hang a strip of fabric between the needles, then knit over it to secure it in place. Then fold the shag around every other stitch.

For variation on this rug design, match the knit fabric to the color of your bathroom, or substitute T-shirt fabric, denim (cut the strips on the bias), knit tights, or fleece.

MATERIALS

- **Six 4-ounce (113.5-gram) skeins worsted-weight yarn in neutral color**
- **60in (150cm)-wide, single jersey-knit fabric in three compatible colors:**

  2¼yd (187.5cm) for border color

  1½yd (135cm) of color A

  1½yd (135cm) of color B

YOU'LL ALSO NEED:

Rotary cutter or cutting shears; size 8 (size 6 Canadian) knitting needles or size to give gauge; and tape measure.

KNITTING TERMS

* **Shag Gauge:**   **16 sts = 4in (10cm)**

                              23 rows = 4in (10cm)

* **Abbreviations:**   **k = knit**

                              st = stitch

                              sts = stitches

Instructions

1. Cut shag strips. Using rotary cutter or shears, cut two 1 x 3in (2.5 x 7.5cm) strips from knit fabric, one along lengthwise grain, and one along crosswise grain. Select the look you prefer, then cut remainder of fabric accordingly. First cut long 1in (2.5cm)-wide strips, then cut those strips into 3in (7.5cm)-long sections. Keep colors separate.

2. Knit rug. Refer to illustration A for schematic of color changes. On size 8 needles, cast on 89 stitches.

Row 1: Knit.

Row 2 (shag st row): K 1, end with yarn in back (illustration B).★ Lay border color fabric strip between needles so it hangs evenly in front and back (illustration C), k 1. Lift back of strip through needles to front (illustration D), k 1, end with yarn in back (illustration E).★ Repeat from ★ to ★ (which will be referred to as K2 combination) to end of row. Repeat rows 1 and 2, eight more times.

Row 19: Knit.

Row 20: K 1, k 11 border color shag sts,★ k 2 combination A color shag sts, k 2 combination B color shag sts,★ repeat from ★ to ★ for 66 sts, k 11 border color shag sts.

Row 21: Knit.

Row 22: K 1, k 11 border color shag sts, k 2 combination A color shag sts, ★ repeat from ★ to ★ for 66 sts, knit 11 border color shag sts. Repeat rows 19 through 22 for 25in (63.5cm), measuring on wrong side, end even-numbered row.

Next row: Knit.

Next row: Same as row 2. Repeat these two rows for 18 rows total. Bind off.

Making the Shag Bath Rug

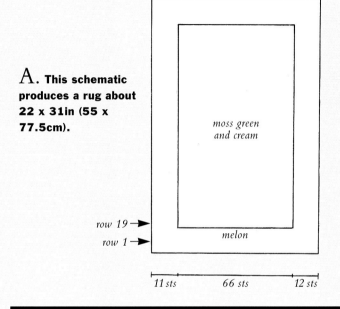

A. This schematic produces a rug about **22 x 31in (55 x 77.5cm).**

moss green and cream

melon

row 19 →

row 1 →

11 sts   66 sts   12 sts

B. Knit one stitch.

C. Lay one fabric shag strip between the needles.

HOW TO MAKE A STRIPED SHAG RUG

To make a striped version of the shag rug, you will need 3½yd (3.15m) of fabric color A, and 2⅞yd (2.58m) of fabric color B. Both fabrics should measure 60in (1.5m)-wide. Start by casting on 89 stitches. Then knit rows 1 to 18 using color A strips on the shag stitch rows. Next knit rows 19 to 36 using color B strips on the shag stitch rows. Continue alternating colors every 18 rows until rug measures 34in (85cm) long.

34in

row 37

B   row 19

A   row 1

89 sts (22in)

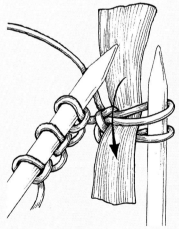

D. Knit one stitch, then flip the back of the strip forward.

E. Knit one stitch to lock the shag in place.

Ribbon Appliqué Shower Mat

Keep your bathroom floor dry with this whimsical shower mat. All you need to get started is a pair of all-purpose waffle piqué towels (or fabric) and washable grosgrain ribbon. This mat features black grosgrain ribbon on white waffle piqué, which coordinates nicely with black and white tiles, but both grosgrain ribbon and piqué are available in a wide range of colors, so this mat is easily customized to the colors of your bathroom. You can also change the letters on the mat to personalize it to your home.

———

For variation on this design, spell out your first name, your family name, or your initials on the mat.

MATERIALS

- **Two 17 x 28in (42.5 x 70cm) waffle piqué towels**
- **4yd (3.6m) ⅞in (2.2cm)-wide washable grosgrain ribbon**

YOU'LL ALSO NEED:

Iron and ironing board; sewing machine; thread to match towels; thread to match ribbon; straight pins; ruler or yardstick; sewing shears.

DESIGNER'S TIP

For variation on the mat's border, make a more elaborate border using two or three colors of ribbon, create a two- or three-tone effect by sewing narrower ribbons on top of wider ones, or make triangle motifs by folding the ribbon back and forth.

Instructions

1. Prepare towels. Cut labels off towels. Press both towels to eliminate packing folds.

2. Establish lettering placement. Determine exact center of towel using ruler or yardstick, then mark with two crossed pins. Determine height of lettering, then mark off with two lines of pins (see illustration A, facing page). Cutting ribbon pieces longer than needed, position central letter first, adjusting as necessary to account for width of flanking letters (i.e., M and O are wider than T or J). Let apex of pointed letters, such as A or W, rise slightly above height of other letters. Pin central letter in place, folding raw ribbon-ends under by ¼in (6mm) at top and bottom, and neatly tucking in any protruding bits. Trap horizontal strokes, like the cross bar of A, under vertical strokes they intersect (illustration B). Pin remaining letters in place, then view from distance to make sure letters look balanced (illustration C).

3. Sew ribbon letters. Thread machine needle with thread to match ribbon and bobbin with color to match piqué. Leave approximately 4in (10cm) extra thread at beginning and end of stitching. Edge-stitch ribbon all around, tucking in turnings carefully with scissor tips as you go. Poke excess thread at start and finish to back side of mat using pin, then knot thread ends.

4. Assemble mat. Pin both towels wrong sides together, matching them at corners. Load machine and bobbin with thread to match piqué. To avoid stitching through bulk of two hems, stitch all around both towels ⅝in (1.6cm) from edges (illustration D).

5. Add ribbon border. Thread needle of machine with thread to match ribbon. Starting at bottom right hand corner of mat, pin ribbon inside double bulk of hems, but covering previous stitching to leave ½in (1.2cm) white border showing (illustration E). Pin slanting miters at corners. Edge stitch around outside and inner edges of ribbon (illustration F). Finish by knotting threads on back and thread ends on hand needle and hide the ends in between the two towels. Press mat.

Making the Ribbon Appliqué Mat

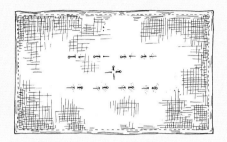

A. **Establish the center of the mat and the height of the letters, then mark with pins.**

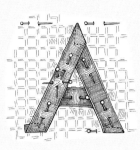

B. **Pin the central letter first, turning under the raw ends and intersecting the pieces.**

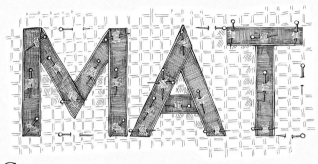

C. **Add the letters on either side of the central letter.**

right side

wrong sides

stitch line (⅝in [1.6cm]) from edge

original hem of towel 1½in (4cm)

D. **Sew the two towels together to form one firm mat.**

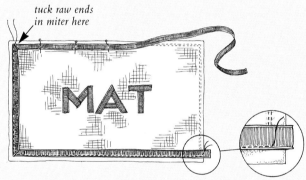

tuck raw ends in miter here

E. **Miter the corners and edge stitch the outer side of the border ribbon.**

edgestitch inner side of ribbon

F. **Then edge stitch the inner side of the border ribbon.**

HOW TO MAKE CURVED LETTERS

Letters made up of straight lines are easy to sew, but letters with curves can be a little more challenging. There are two options, both of which are quick and easy: press the curves into the ribbon using a steam iron, or fold and pleat the ribbon, then secure with hand basting. For longer words, use narrower ribbon.

31

vanity

Plastic Makeup Bag

This makeup bag introduces you to the adventure of sewing with plastic. Plastic's inherent static charges mean that you don't need to pin the layers together before stitching, and because plastic will never fray, you can sew the entire project right-side out, then simply trim away the seam allowances. Start by attaching a zipper to two squares of plastic vinyl, then join the plastic shapes to one another with simple machine stitching. When you've finished sewing, trim the seam allowances close to the stitching to accentuate the corners of this contemporary shape.

—

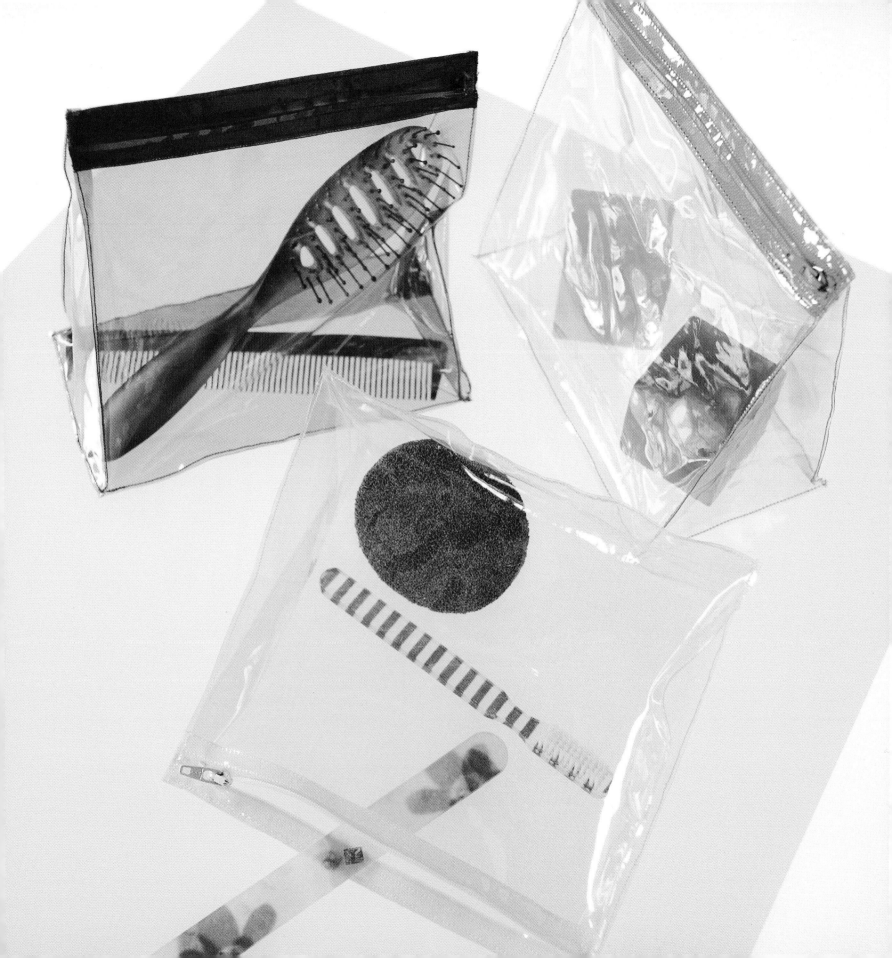

Plastic makeup bags are excellent for the bathroom, but you will also find dozens of other uses for them. They are tailor-made for travel, as they can be made as large or as small as necessary.

MATERIALS

Yields one 7in (18cm) wedge-shaped bag

- **¼yd (23cm) 45 to 60in (112.5 to 150cm)-wide tinted vinyl plastic**
- **7in (18cm) zipper in coordinating color**
- **Matching thread**

YOU'LL ALSO NEED:

gusset pattern (see page 120); sewing machine and zipper foot attachment; rotary cutter; self-healing cutting mat; quilter's acrylic grid ruler; and craft utility knife with new blade.

SEWING TIP

Does vinyl cling to your sewing machine bed and presser foot, instead of gliding through? For smooth sewing, try a Teflon foot—it will touch down on the vinyl without sticking to it. To "unstick" steel or plastic feet, affix a small piece of masking tape to the underside. Plastic machine beds will also lose their "stick" if you tape copier paper over them; cover all areas except the plate and feed dogs.

Instructions

Note: Sew vinyl pieces wrong sides together, so seams show on right side.

1. Cut five pattern pieces. Photocopy and enlarge gusset pattern (see page 120). Lay vinyl flat on gridded cutting mat. Using rotary cutter and acrylic cutting guide, cut following pieces: two 7½in (19.2cm) squares, one 4 x 7½in (10 x 19.2cm) rectangle, and two gussets (slip photocopy of gusset pattern between vinyl and mat).

2. Sew inset zipper to vinyl square. Place zipper face down on one vinyl square, allowing ¼in (6mm) between tape edge and top edge of vinyl. Zig-zag other long edge of zipper tape through both layers. Turn square over. Using zipper foot, stitch as close to zipper teeth as possible on both sides (see illustration A, facing page). Using craft knife, cut opening in vinyl directly above zipper teeth; make single continuous cut, without stopping or lifting blade from surface; do not cut all the way to edges. Run zipper open and closed a few times to make sure vinyl is cut clear through.

3. Join squares and gussets. Lay square with zipper tab right side down. Place gusset on one side edge, tapered end toward zipper; stitch ¼in (6mm) from edge. Using scissors, trim seam allowance (including zipper tape) as close to stitching as possible. Repeat process to join second gusset to opposite side edge. Repeat to join second vinyl square to remaining gusset edges (illustration B).

4. Sew bottom and top. Lay vinyl rectangle flat, and stand bag upright on it. Sew bag edges to corresponding base edges, long edges first, making ¼in (6mm) seams; trim close to stitching as you complete each seam. At top of bag, align edges and press together. Stitch through all layers, catching top edge of zipper tape in seam. Trim vinyl seam allowance even with zipper tape (illustration C).

Making the Plastic Makeup Bag

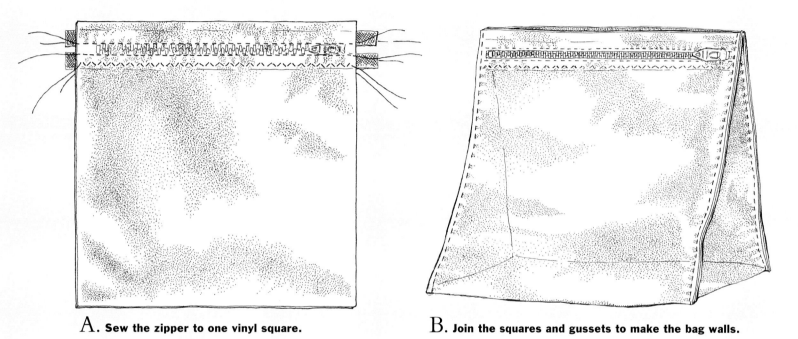

A. **Sew the zipper to one vinyl square.**

B. **Join the squares and gussets to make the bag walls.**

C. **Join the rectangular base and stitch the top closed.**

Footstool
with Piqué Slipcover

You won't need to purchase fabric to make this tufted cushion slipcover. The

slipcover is made from five white waffle piqué towels, which measure 17 x 28in

(42.5 by 70cm). Four towels make up the side panels and top, while the fifth

towel forms the cover for a button-tufted cushion filled with washable batting.

—

Patches of hook-and-loop tape hold this piqué slipcover on its ordinary wooden stool. Hook and loop spots also connect the button-tufted cushion to the top of the slipcover.

MATERIALS

- One rectangular wooden stool, no more than 17in (42.5cm) high or wide
- Five 17 x 28in (42.5 x 70cm) waffle piqué towels
- Polyester cushion to fit top of footstool or four thicknesses of 1in (2.5cm)-thick polyester batting cut to size
- Four 1in (2.5cm) white hook-and-loop patches or 4 pieces hook-and-loop tape cut into 1in (2.5cm) squares
- Nine ¾in (1.8cm) cover-your-own button kit

YOU'LL ALSO NEED:

Tape measure or ruler; marking pencil; sewing machine; white thread; sewing needle; sewing shears; iron and ironing board.

DESIGNER'S TIP

The slipcover shown here conceals a small but sturdy wood nesting table, but a little rectangular stool or a small Parson's table will work equally well. Adapt the measurements in our instructions to fit your own stool.

Instructions

1. Calculate size of footstool. Measure top of stool. Here, the stool top measures 15 x 11½in (37.5 x 28.5cm). Measure height; ours measures 17in (42.5cm) high (see illustration A, facing page). Record measurements.

2. Press side pleats. Form four skirt panels by pressing in sides of two towels to match 15in (37.5cm) measurement (illustration B), and two to match 11½in (28.5cm) measurement (illustration C). Hems on towels will be used as bottom hems on panels. Cut all four towels at 17½in (43.7 cm).

3. Sew top for footstool. From leftover fabric, cut two 8½ x 12½in (21.7 x 31.2cm) for footstool top. Join pieces using ½in (1.2cm) seam; piece will fit top of footstool plus ½in (1.2cm) seam allowance all around (illustration D).

4. Make buttons and tabs. Cover nine buttons with fabric scraps. To make tabs, cut four 3½in (8.2cm)-square pieces from leftover fabric. Fold in half, then stitch using ½in (1.2cm) seam. Center seam, then press seam open. Stitch pointed ends, then trim (illustration E). Turn each tab right side out. Stitch across raw edges to prevent unraveling. Machine-stitch spot of hook-and-loop tape on underside of tabs (button will cover stitching on top of tab).

5. Place and stitch tabs. Mark 7in (18cm) down side of wide towel panels with pin. Pin tab underneath pressed crease so 2in (5cm) shows beyond edge of skirt (illustration F). Sew hem down creases of both sides of widest towels, catching tabs as you stitch. Leave creases on narrower towels unhemmed, as they will under-lap and continue around corners.

6. Join side panels to top. With right sides together, pin wide panels of skirt to top piece. Double check fit on footstool (pieces should line up exactly at corners), then stitch (illustration G). Repeat process to stitch narrow panels to top piece; pressed-in creases should reach corners of stool, and unhemmed sides of panels should extend around corners to form an open, flap at corners (illustration H).

7. Add hook-and-loop fastenings. Mark skirt and tabs for

Making the Footstool

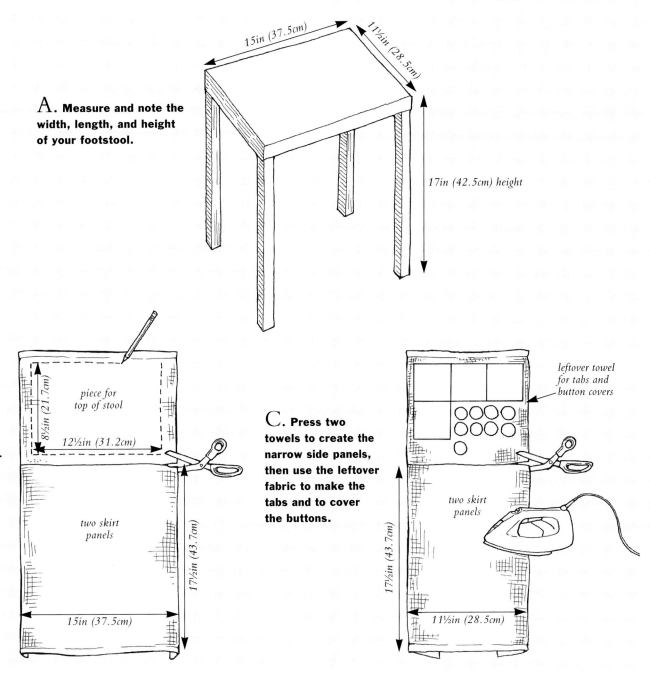

A. **Measure and note the width, length, and height of your footstool.**

15in (37.5cm)

11½in (28.5cm)

17in (42.5cm) height

B. **Press two towels to create the wide side panels, then use the leftover fabric for the footstool top.**

piece for top of stool

8½in (21.7cm)

12½in (31.2cm)

two skirt panels

17½in (43.7cm)

15in (37.5cm)

C. **Press two towels to create the narrow side panels, then use the leftover fabric to make the tabs and to cover the buttons.**

leftover towel for tabs and button covers

two skirt panels

17½in (43.7cm)

11½in (28.5cm)

If your stool is too large for covering with towels, you can make a fitted slipcover using white piqué yard goods or any other washable fabric. Follow these instructions, but add hems where needed.

matched pairs of hook-and-loop patches, and then stitch in place. Attach buttons to outside of tabs, covering stitches. Remove skirt from footstool, then sew five hook-and-loop spots or patches of hook-and-loop tape on top piece; position four pieces 2in (5cm) in from each corner and one piece in center (illustration I).

8. Make seat cushion. Using fifth towel, cut piece equal to measurement of footstool top plus ¾in (1.8cm) all around for seam allowance. Taper corners by shaving off ¼in (6mm) at adjoining seam allowances so corners will not stick out. Before joining both sides of cushion together, sew on hook-and-loop patches 2½in (6.2cm) from corners; positioning should match patches on top of footstool (illustration J). Stitch cushion pieces together, right sides together and using ½in (1.2cm) seam allowance; leave 6in (15cm) opening at center of one side for turning. Trim corners. Turn cushion right side out. Fill with fiberfill or batting, then slipstitch opening closed.

9. Tuft cushion. Mark center of cushion with crossed pins. Match up cushion with hook-and-loop patches on top of footstool slipcover. Using long needle and double thread, sew buttons at center, pulling through to underside to create tufted effect (illustration K). Place pillow on seat, matching up hook-and-loop patches to keep cushion in place (illustration L).

Making the Top and Tabs

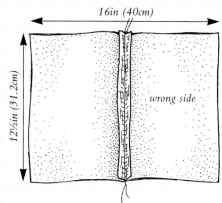

16in (40cm)

12½in (31.2cm)

wrong side

D. **Join the two top pieces together, centering the seam.**

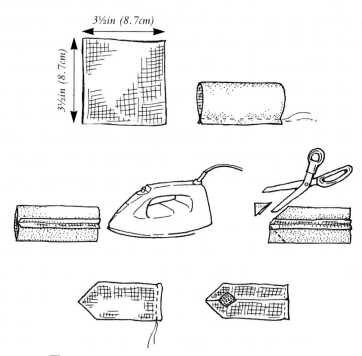

3½in (8.7cm)

3½in (8.7cm)

E. **To make the tabs, cut four square pieces, fold in half, stitch, sew the points, trim, and turn right side out. Stitch across the raw edges, then add a spot of hook-and-loop tape to the underside.**

Finishing the Footstool

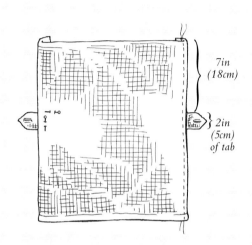

7in (18cm)

2in (5cm) of tab

F. **Pin the tabs underneath the pressed creases. Stitch the side hem to hold the tabs in place.**

G. **Attach the panels to the slipcover top, wide panels first.**

H. **Sew on the narrow panels so they wrap around the corners under the wide panels.**

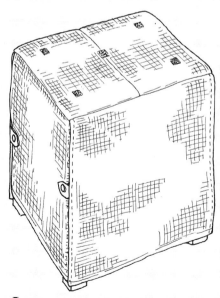

I. **Sew five hook-and-loop patches on top of footstool.**

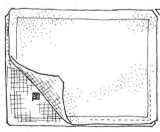

J. **Using the fifth towel, cut a piece equal to the measurement of the footstool top plus ¾in (1.8cm) all around. Trim corners to reduce bulk.**

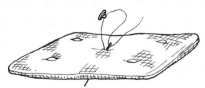

K. **With a long needle and double thread, sew buttons to tuft the cushion.**

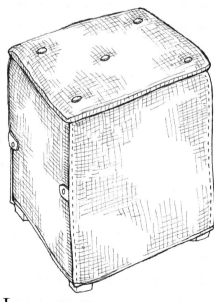

L. **Place pillow on seat, matching up hook-and-loop patches to keep it in place.**

43

Drawstring Makeup Pouch

This lined pouch, designed to hold makeup or bathroom supplies such as cotton balls, will dress up a shelf or vanity counter. This bag comprises two circles of fabric, using one circle for the outside and a contrasting circle for the lining, held together with soft, silky cord. To give the bag a sturdy base, we trapped a plastic lid from a coffee can between the circles of fabric.

———

Drawstring pouches with plastic bottoms can be made in various sizes. A small bag is great for storing rings or small pieces of jewelry, while a larger bag can accommodate an assortment of hair care products.

MATERIALS

- **18in (45cm) fabric for outside of bag**
- **18in (45cm) fabric for bag lining**
- **Plastic coffee can lid for base**
- **1½yd (135cm) silk cord**

YOU'LL ALSO NEED:

Marking pencil; tape measure; scissors; sewing machine with buttonhole capability and zipper foot; matching thread; safety pin or bodkin for threading cord; iron and ironing board; and seam sealant.

Instructions

1. Cut fabric. Mark 18in (45cm) circle on wrong side of outer fabric, using 9in (23cm) length of string tied to pencil to draw circumference. Cut circle from outer fabric, then repeat with lining fabric.

2. Mark and sew buttonholes. Fold outer circle in half along grain. Mark edges of folds with pins (see illustration A, facing page). Measure in from raw edges 1¾in (4.3cm) along both folds and mark. Open fabric and mark ¾in (18mm) buttonhole with pin placed parallel to edge. With matching thread, machine-sew both buttonholes on outer fabric only (illustration B).

3. Sew circles together. Place both circles right sides together, matching grains. Sew around edge, allowing ¼in (6mm) seams and leaving 4in (10cm) opening for turning (illustration C). Turn right side out and press.

4. Add base. Slide plastic coffee can lid in through opening. Center it between both fabrics in circle, flat side down against outer fabric, and pin in place. Using zipper foot, stitch around plastic disc from lining side (illustration D). Slip-stitch opening closed and press.

5. Sew casing. Stitch all around, through both fabrics, 1¼in (3.5cm) from outer edge (illustration E). Stitch second line ½in (1.2cm) closer to center of circle, making sure buttonholes lie between two rows of stitching.

6. Add drawstring cords. Divide silk cord into two equal pieces. Treat cord ends with seam sealant. Let dry. Using safety pin or bodkin, thread one piece of cord through channel created in step 5; enter and exit from the same buttonhole. Tie ends of cord together in knot. Repeat for second cord using second buttonhole (illustration F). Hide knots in casing, as shown in illustration G, or tie cords at each buttonhole and knot ends individually. To close bag, pull cords from opposite sides at the same time.

Making the Drawstring Pouch

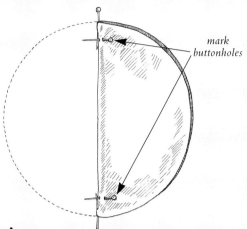

A. **Fold the outer circle in two along the grain and mark the edge of the fold with pins. Use pins across the fold to mark the buttonholes.**

mark buttonholes

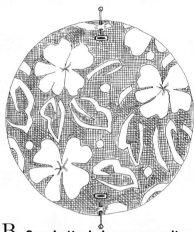

B. **Sew buttonholes on opposite sides of the outer fabric.**

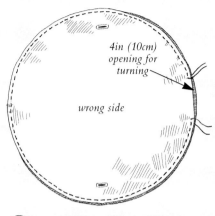

4in (10cm) opening for turning

wrong side

C. **Place both circles right sides together. Sew around the edge, leaving an opening for turning.**

D. **Slide a plastic lid in through the opening, center it in the circle, and stitch around it from the lining side. Slipstitch the opening closed.**

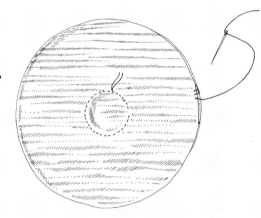

E. **Sew two lines of stitching through both fabrics, positioning the buttonholes between the rows of stitching.**

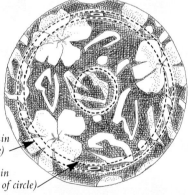

1st line of stitching (1¼in [3.5cm] from outer edge)

2nd line of stitching (½in [1.2cm] closer to center of circle)

F. **To make drawstring cords, thread cord in one buttonhole, all the way around the circle, and out the same buttonhole. Repeat with second cord in second buttonhole and knot as shown.**

G. **To close the bag, pull both the cords from both sides.**

47

Vanity Chair Cushion

These stylish cushions use three different colors of fabric to achieve a bold but tasteful geometric pattern. If your budget is tight, search for bargains at the remnants table, as one pillow requires less than a yard or meter of each color fabric. The ties at the back of the cushions make the covers easy to remove for laundering. Ties also enable you to stack and connect the cushions to themselves or to the posts of a chair.

———

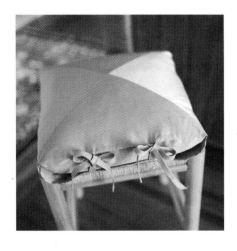

Each cushion uses three fabric colors, so try combining pastels, primary colors, or a classic combination of black, white, and red. For a relaxed, casual look, combine a selection of denim shades, or three variations of striped shirting.

MATERIALS

- ■ ½yd (45cm) fabric color A (white)
- ■ ⅔yd (60cm) fabric color B (gold)
- ■ ½yd (45cm) fabric color C (blue)
- ■ 16in square (40cm) polyester fiberfill knife-edge pillow form

YOU WILL ALSO NEED:

Paper for making patterns; ruler; marking pencil; sewing shears; straight pins; sewing machine; matching thread; iron and ironing board.

SEWING TIP

It's easy to make copies of patterns, simply by tracing around them on pieces cut from a roll of brown wrapping paper. If the wrapping paper curls, press it lightly to flatten it.

Instructions

1. Make basic pattern. Mark and cut one piece of paper 16in (40cm) square. Taper corners by marking dot ¾in (1.8cm) in from each corner. Mark 4in (10cm) in from each corner along edge of square. Draw line from corner dots to 4in marks (see illustration A, facing page). Mark grain direction with arrows, and mark right or wrong side. This square is the basic cushion cover pattern.

2. Make facing pattern. Trace tapered cushion cover pattern, then cut off rectangle (illustration B) measuring 4in x 16in (10cm x 40cm). Divide the original 16in (40cm) width into thirds and notch where ties will be attached.

3. Make pattern for sides. On basic pattern piece, draw lines diagonally, from corner to corner, dividing pattern into four sections. Mark with letters for fabric colors, then cut apart (illustration C). When you lay these triangular patterns on fabric for cutting, add ½in (1.2cm) seam allowance on all sides (illustration D).

4. Prepare and cut fabric. Press all three fabrics. Place pattern pieces on folded (2 layers) appropriate color fabrics. Allow space for ½in (1.2cm) seam allowance on all sides. Lay pattern for facings in fabric B, adding seam allowance. Mark two pieces 12in x 2in (30cm x 5cm) for ties on fabric B (four ties in all). Lay pattern pieces on fabric, on grain, in most economical way. Cut pieces and sort into piles, one for each side of cushion cover.

Making the Vanity Chair Cushion

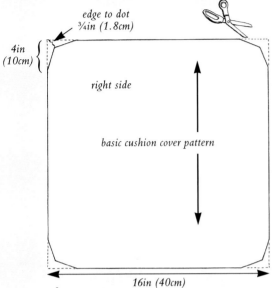

edge to dot
¾in (1.8cm)

4in (10cm)

right side

basic cushion cover pattern

16in (40cm)

A. Draw the basic pattern piece and taper the corners.

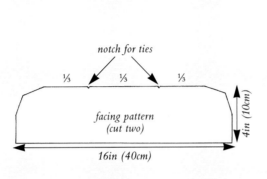

notch for ties

⅓   ⅓   ⅓

facing pattern (cut two)

4in (10cm)

16in (40cm)

B. Cut the facing pattern using a copy of the tapered cushion pattern, then add notches to locate the ties.

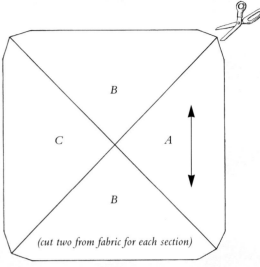

B

C   *A*

B

(cut two from fabric for each section)

C. For the cushion sections, draw and cut diagonals from corner to corner.

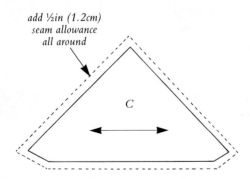

add ½in (1.2cm) seam allowance all around

C

D. Before cutting the pieces, add ½in (1.2cm) seam allowance all around.

E. Cut the tie strips and press in one end and two long edges.

right side

F. Press the tie strip in half lengthwise.

G. Stitch around the ties and press.

For variation on this design, divide the basic pattern into three stripes. To make a reversible cushion, sew stripes on one side and the triangular pattern on the other.

5. Make ties. Press in ¼in (6mm) to wrong side at one end of tie strip. Leave other end raw as it will be trapped in facing seam. Fold strip in half lengthwise, wrong sides together. Press. Turn long raw edges in to meet at center creaseline. Press so new fold lines are on top of each other. Choose matching thread and edge stitch around ties. Press flat (illustration G).

6. Sew cushion covers. Sew fabric C to fabric B along diagonal seam with ½in (1.2cm) seam allowance. Press seam open. Sew second piece of fabric B to diagonal seam of fabric A. Press open. Lay the two completed seams on top of each other, right sides facing, and sew along diagonal to join all four pieces into a square. Press seams. Repeat for back cover.

7. Place ties. Pin ties onto notches on right sides of cushion cover front and back, with raw edges matching, and with ties lying toward body of cushion (illustration H).

8. Sew facings. Press in ¼in (6mm) hem, then a second hem, to form small hem on straight edge of both facing pieces. Topstitch hems. Place one facing on top of each cushion square with right sides together. Pin, then sew along top edge only, catching ties in seam (illustration I). Turn covers to wrong side, lifting facings to top. Press facing seams toward covers.

9. Sew cushion cover together. Pin front and back cushion covers with right sides together and facings opened toward top. Stitch around three sides, leaving top edge open (illustration J).

10. Finish cushion. Trim corners. Turn cushion cover right side out and press. Fold facings to inside. Insert pillow form, then hide pillow edge by tucking behind one facing. Push form well into corners and fluff up. Knot ties and arrange cushion on chair (illustration K).

SEWING TIPS

When you lay out pattern pieces on cloth, use weights to keep patterns in place while you work.

When making patterns, it helps to identify the color of the fabric with a vivid magic marker, or with a small sticky label with an identifying letter. Place labels at upper left hand side of each piece before cutting to eliminate mistakes.

Finishing the Vanity Chair Cushion

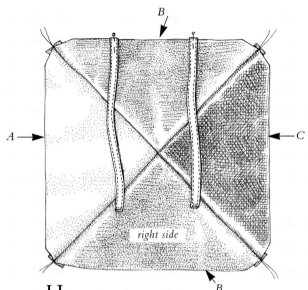

H. **Pin the ties in place.**

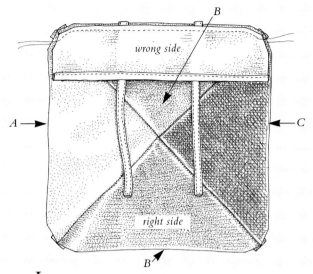

I. **With right sides together, sew the long edge of the facing to the cushion cover, catching the ties in the seam.**

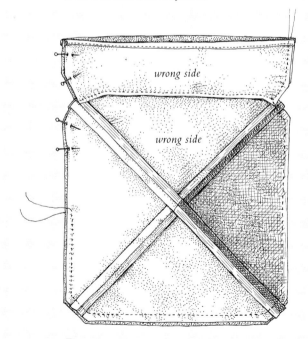

J. **Open the facings and place the right sides of both covers together. Stitch around three sides, leaving the top open.**

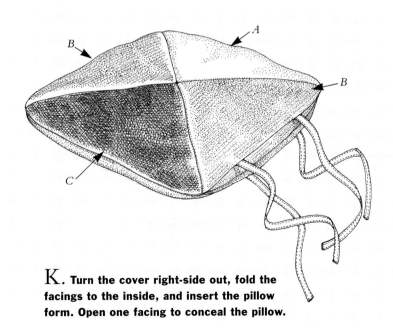

K. **Turn the cover right-side out, fold the facings to the inside, and insert the pillow form. Open one facing to conceal the pillow.**

Scented Hangers

These sweet-scented satin-covered hangers will sparkle up any vanity. We made them in vivid contemporary colors with trimmings of bright multicolored ribbons. Satins come in many hues and you need very little for one hanger, so be bold and unexpected in your color choices. We used two different ribbons crossed on the satin body of the hanger, with a third color covering the hook.

———

Ribbon can be randomly placed to give an artlessly casual effect, though more than three colors quickly get out of control. Instead of adding more colors, look for ribbon with metallic accents, or with beaded edges.

MATERIALS

- **Wooden dress hanger with screw-in hook**
- **¼yd (23cm) 45in (112.5cm)-wide silk or satin**
- **¼yd (23cm) 1in (2.5cm) medium-weight polyester or cotton batting**
- **1½yd (135cm) each, 3 colors satin ribbon in assorted widths, no wider than ½in (12mm)**
- **1oz (28.4g) dried lavender**
- **A few drops essential oil of lavender**

YOU'LL ALSO NEED:

Marking pencil; ruler; sewing shears; sewing machine; matching threads; needle; fabric glue or double sided tape; and sewing needle.

Instructions

1. Make fragrance. Put lavender flowers in small bowl. Sprinkle with essential oil. Stir. Let stand few hours until oil is absorbed.

2. Lay out fabric. Remove hook from hanger and set aside. Place hanger on wrong side of silk or satin and trace with marking pencil (see illustration A, facing page). Remove hanger and draw line 1¼in (3.1cm) beyond outline all around (illustration B).

3. Cut hanger cover. Cut one half of cover, then fold in half to ensure symmetry before cutting second half. Find location for notch using hanger as guide, then make notch at edge of top center. On bottom edge, notch 6in (15cm) on either side of center to create opening for turning. Pin this shape to remaining fabric right sides together and cut a second identical piece.

4. Sew hanger cover. Starting ⅛in (3mm) from top center notch, machine stitch both pieces together, right sides facing, with ⅜in (1cm) seams; stitch around curved ends to notch (illustration C). Repeat in opposite direction. Trim seams and clip curves, then turn cover right side out.

5. Prepare batting. Cut batting into rectangle 8in (20cm) by 2in (5cm) longer than hanger. Stir lavender flowers and sprinkle over batting. Center hanger at bottom edge of batting (illustration D). Fold batting around hanger, pulling tightly and easing over curves. Trim excess batting. Secure batting by whip-stitching raw edges at sides and bottom (illustration E). Make hole in batting with hook of hanger so you can insert it later.

6. Put cover on hanger. Undo a few stitches at bottom and gently push batting-covered hanger into cover, compressing batting as necessary. Slip-stitch bottom edge closed (illustration F).

7. Wrap and replace hook. Put small amount of glue or piece of double-sided tape onto screw end of hook. Tightly wrap ribbon around hook, overlapping turns so no metal shows. Catch end of ribbon in glue or double-sided tape, anchoring it near screw. When dry, screw hook through batting into hanger.

8. Add ribbon decoration. Tuck end of ribbon between slip-stitches on bottom edge of hanger cover, about 1in (2.5cm) from center using points of scissors. Wind ribbon over hanger cover to end, pin to top seam, then wind to other end (illustration G), pin, and wind back to start. Cut, leaving ½in (1.2cm) end to tuck into same space between slip-stitching. Secure ribbon with hand stitches in matching thread at both ends of hanger cover. Remove pins. Repeat with second ribbon, winding over previous ribbon and placing it between slanting crosses. To finish, tie bow at base of hook (illustration H).

Making the Scented Hangers

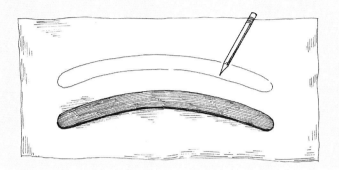

A. Place the hanger on the wrong side of the fabric and draw around it.

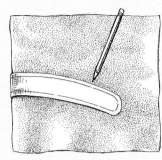

B. Draw the cutting line outside the hanger outline, cut half the shape, and fold it to ensure symmetry.

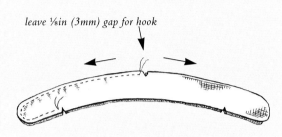

leave ⅛in (3mm) gap for hook

C. Cut two symmetrical shapes, notch, and machine-sew around the pieces, leaving an opening for turning.

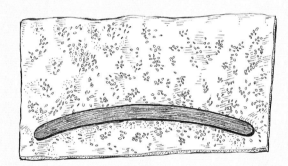

D. Sprinkle prepared lavender flowers over batting, center the hanger, and fold the batting over the hanger.

E. Tuck in the batting edges and secure it with whip stitches.

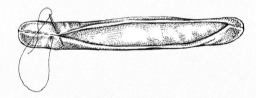

F. Undo a few stiches and push the hanger into the cover. Slipstitch to close the opening.

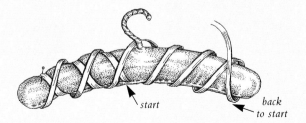

start

back to start

G. Wind one color of ribbon trimming over the hanger and secure with hand stitches.

H. Wind the contrasting ribbon over the hanger, stitch the end, and tie a pretty bow.

57

Reversible Tissue Slipcase

This reversible slipcase makes a pretty display for facial tissues on your vanity counter. The slipcase is designed like a flattened box, and the sides and ends "wrap" around and conceal the tissues. Ribbon ties hold the "box" closed. Because the slipcase is reversible, it features ties on both sides. Alternatively, you can eliminate the second set of ties, but this means the slipcase will no longer be reversible.

———

To "wrap" your tissues, fold in the short ends, followed by the long sides. Then tie the "box" closed.

MATERIALS

- ¼yd (23cm) 45in-60in (112.5cm-150cm)-wide fabric (fabric A)
- ¼yd (23cm) 45in-60in (112.5cm-150cm)-wide fabric (fabric B)
- 1¾yd (157.5cm) ½-1in (1.2cm to 2.5cm)-wide ribbon for trimming (ribbon A)
- 2yd (1.8m) ¼-¾in (6mm to 1.8cm)-wide ribbon for fabric A ties (ribbon B)
- 2yd (1.8m) ¼-¾in (6mm to 1.8cm)-wide ribbon for fabric B ties (ribbon C)

YOU'LL ALSO NEED:

Tape measure or ruler; marking pencil; sewing shears; sewing machine; pins; matching threads; and box of tissues.

Instructions

1. Cut center body, side pieces, and ribbon ties. Cut fabric A into strip 20½ x 5½in (52.1 x 13.7cm) wide. Cut fabric B to same size. These long strips will form base of tissue slipcase. For side pieces, cut two strips of both fabrics measuring 10½ x 5½in (26.7 x 13.7cm) wide. For ties, cut six 10½in (26.7cm) lengths of ribbon.

2. Sew side sections. Position two contrasting side pieces together, right sides facing, then stitch along one long side (see illustration A, facing page). Press seam open (illustration B). Repeat for second side.

3. Add trim to side sections. On right side, topstitch edge of one ribbon (ribbon A) to each short end of joined fabric rectangles from step 2; majority of ribbon width should extend off fabric (illustration C). Fold fabric rectangles right sides together and stitch second long side, trapping raw ends of ribbon (illustration D) inside. Turn sleeve right side out, fold ribbon over raw edge of fabric and topstitch through top layer to bottom layer to form flat, two-sided piece (illustration E).

4. Cut and place ties. Divide ribbons B and C each into four even pieces. Measure 7½in (19.2cm) from ends of long central piece of fabric A, and pin ribbons, alternating sides, on right side

Making the Tissue Slipcase

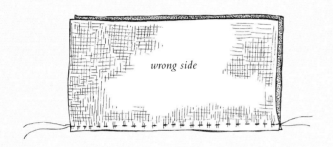

A. Lay the two contrasting side pieces right sides together and stitch along one long side.

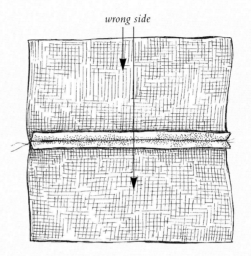

wrong side

B. Press the seam open.

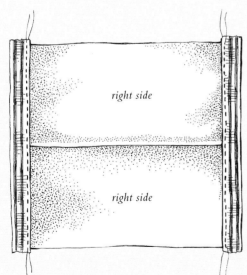

right side

right side

C. Topstitch ribbon A to the short ends so most of the ribbon width extends off the fabric.

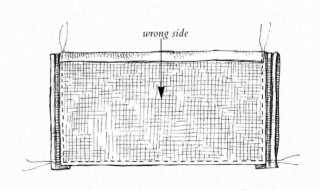

wrong side

D. Fold the rectangles and stitch along the second long side, trapping the ribbon ends.

This soft-sculpture tissue dispenser can hold about one-half of a large box of tissues.

of fabric so that ¼in (6mm) extends beyond long edge of fabric (illustration F).

5. Sew center section. Pin and sew long central piece of fabric B to fabric A, right sides together as in step 3, taking care not to stitch through ribbon ties except where pinned. Turn right side out and topstitch ribbon trim as before (illustration G).

6. Finish tissue slipcase. Measure 5in (12.5cm) in from ribbon-trimmed ends on both sides of long central piece, and pin side pieces in place on outer sides so fabric B sides are facing and ribbon C is trapped inside. With thread matching fabric A, edge-stitch sides to center section (illustration H).

7. Tie slipcase closed. Place tissues in center of center section and fold the two short ends over tissues first (illustrations I, J, and K). Then tie ribbons into bows. Then fold over long edges (illustration L) and tie slipcase closed (illustration M). Space left in middle between edges and ribbons should be perfectly-sized for removing one tissue at a time.

Finishing the Tissue Slipcase

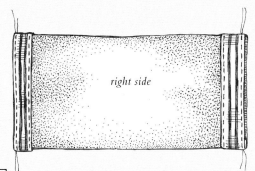

right side

E. **Turn the sleeve right side out and topstitch the top edge of the trim ribbon to itself.**

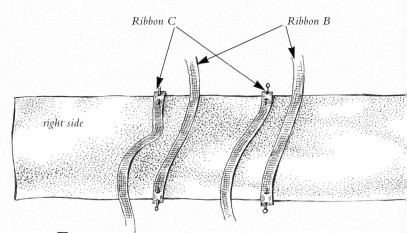

Ribbon C   *Ribbon B*

right side

F. **Pin the ribbons to the center section as shown.**

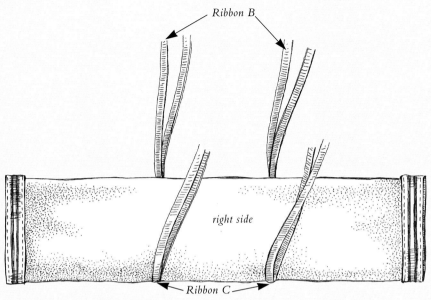

Ribbon B

right side

Ribbon C

G. **Stitch both center pieces together and add a ribbon trim, taking care not to stitch through the tie ribbons except where pinned.**

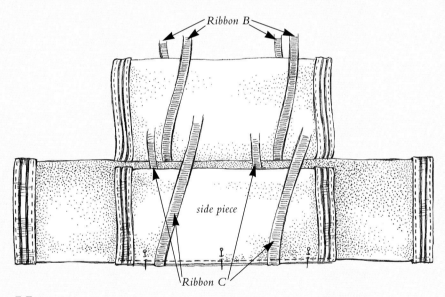

Ribbon B

side piece

Ribbon C

H. **Pin the side pieces onto the center section so two of the ribbon C ties are trapped inside. Edge-stitch the sides in place.**

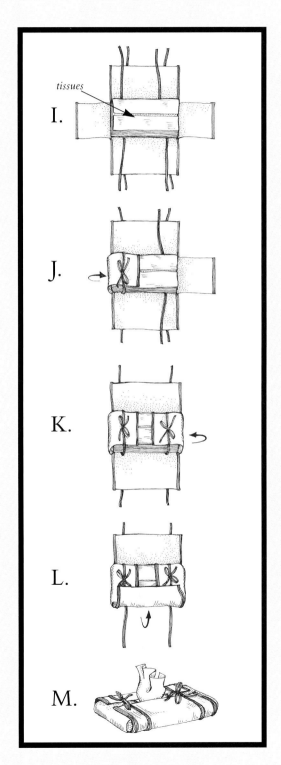

tissues

I.

J.

K.

L.

M.

63

windows and walls

Shower Curtain with Photo Transfer Accents

The trick to making this beautiful shower curtain at home revolves around transfer medium, which lets you make "prints" from one piece of patterned fabric, then transfer those "prints" to a plain white shower curtain. To get started, you'll need to select a fabric with a repeated motif (here the fabric is covered with butterflies). Next, make color copies of selected images on the fabric. Then use the transfer medium to "print" the images onto the plain shower curtain. Finish the curtain with top and bottom bands and ties cut from the original patterned fabric.

———

Transferring the images takes about 24 hours and should be done before adding the bands, as the transferring process involves soaking and machine washing.

MATERIALS

- **2yd (180cm) 72in (180cm)-wide translucent fabric (for shower curtain)**
- **1¼yd (1.1m) 45in (1.1m)-wide printed fabric (for bands, ties, and transferred images)**
- **Transfer medium**

YOU'LL ALSO NEED:

Sewing shears or rotary cutter and cutting mat; marking pencil; tape measure; yardstick or right angled ruler; sewing machine; matching thread; scissors; double-sided tape; iron and ironing board; access to washing machine; access to color photocopier; and chopstick or knitting needle (for turning ties).

Instructions

1. Cut shower curtain. With rotary cutter or shears, cut piece measuring 72in (180cm) square from translucent fabric.

2. Cut bands and ties. From printed fabric cut two bands measuring 5½ x 37in (13.7 x 92.5cm). Bands will be joined at side "B" into one band for top of curtain, so check that design matches at center seam (see illustration A). For bottom band, cut two bands measuring 10 x 37in (25 x 92.5cm), checking that design matches along "E" sides and join as before. For ties, cut as

many 1¾in (4.3cm)-wide strips as needed to yield one long strip measuring 5¾yd (5.16m) long once strips are sewn together. This 5¾yd (5.16m) strip will be cut into 24 individual ties.

3. Sew bands and ties. Join two top edge band pieces using ½in (1.2cm) seam at center. Repeat to join two bottom band pieces. Join strip for ties with ¼in (6mm) seams. Press seams open. Fold strip in half lengthwise, right sides facing, pin, then stitch ¼in (6mm) from raw edges (illustration B). Press seams open, keeping seam centered in strip (illustration C). Mark with pencil every 8½in (21.2cm), sew across each mark, and cut ⅛in (3mm) beyond stitches (illustration D). Using chopstick or knitting needle, turn each tie right side out. Press each tie, keeping seam centered. Sew ties together in pairs, one on top of the other, along raw edges (illustration E) to yield 12 pairs of ties; raw edges will be trapped in seam at top of curtain.

4. Photocopy, cut out, and transfer accents. Make color photocopies, as desired, using bands of trim fabric. If letters or numbers are involved, or motif direction is critical, use the "mirror image" function on color copier. Cut out each motif. Pin top and bottom bands to curtain to gauge overall design, then fasten accents to curtain using double-sided tape. Keep in mind that accents will be reversed when positioned on fabric. Transfer accents to shower curtain following manufacturer's instructions. Trim the color copy to size, then place face up on waxed paper. Brush on thick coat of medium. Place copy on fabric, coated side down, and cover with paper towel. Roll medium bottle across copy, then remove paper towel. Let dry 24 to 48 hours. Wet copy using sponge, then let set 2 minutes. Use damp sponge to remove paper backing from image, then let dry overnight.

Cutting the Shower Curtain

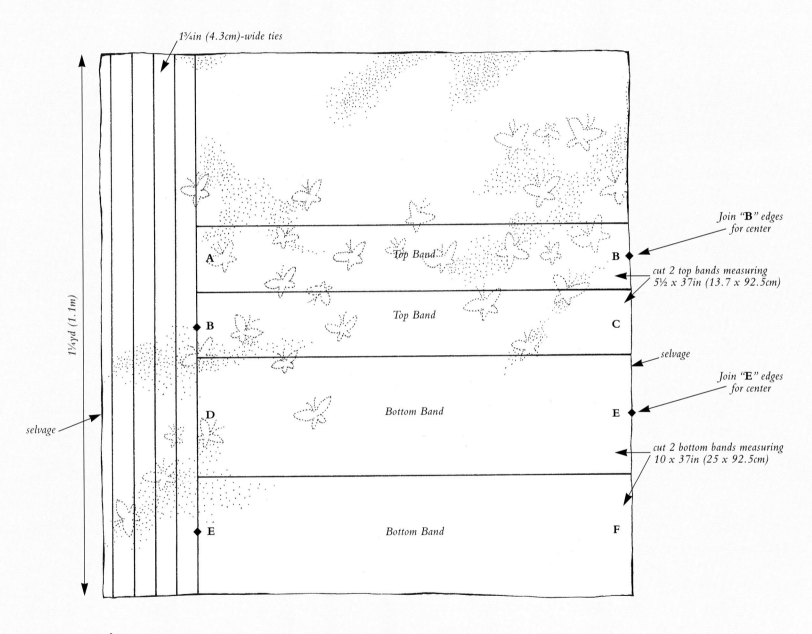

1¾in (4.3cm)-wide ties

1¼yd (1.1m)

selvage

A

Top Band

B

Join "**B**" edges
for center

cut 2 top bands measuring
5½ x 37in (13.7 x 92.5cm)

B

Top Band

C

selvage

D

Bottom Band

E

Join "**E**" edges
for center

cut 2 bottom bands measuring
10 x 37in (25 x 92.5cm)

E

Bottom Band

F

A. Lay out the trim bands and ties on the patterned fabric.

For variation on this design, select a fabric with flowers, fish, geometric shapes, or the like.

5. Sew shower curtain. Starting ½in (1.2cm) in from the two side edges on the wrong side, pin 12 pairs of ties evenly spaced, raw edges matching. (As shower curtain measures 72in [180cm] on all sides, it does not matter which side you work on, but keep in mind that this side will become the top edge of the shower curtain.) Position top trim band on top of ties, right side down and trapping ties in between, then stitch across top, ½in (1.2cm) from edge (illustration F). Press seam allowances of both fabrics toward curtain fabric (illustration G), then topstitch on curtain ⅛in (3mm) from seam to prevent curtain fabric from showing along top seam. Turn top trim band to right side of curtain, and press across topstitch seam. On raw long edge of trim band, press ¼in (6mm) to wrong side, then pin pressed edge of band to curtain. Thread machine so top thread matches band and bobbin thread matches curtain. Topstitch pressed edge, then remove pins (illustration H). Repeat process using bottom trim band at bottom of curtain, but eliminate ties.

6. Finish curtain. Press ¼in (6mm) hem twice to wrong side, at sides of curtain, then topstitch with matching thread. Change thread when hemming sides of trim bands. If pressing curtain, avoid photo transferred images, as heat can damage them. To hang curtain, tie knots on shower curtain over rod (illustration I).

Making the Ties

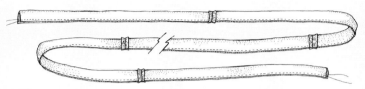

B. **Join the strip for the ties. Fold the strip in half lengthwise and stitch.**

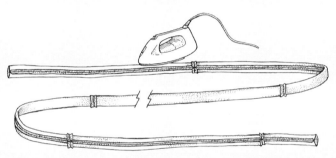

C. **Press the seam open, keeping it centered in the strip.**

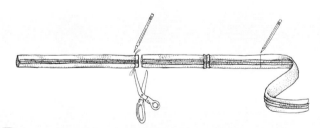

D. **Mark the strip every 8½in (21.2cm).**

E. **Sew the ties together in pairs along the raw edges.**

Assembling the Shower Curtain

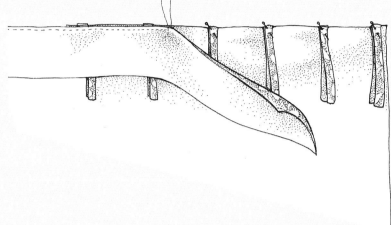

F. Pin 12 pairs of ties, evenly spaced, along the wrong side of the curtain top. Trap the ties with the trim band, and stitch in place.

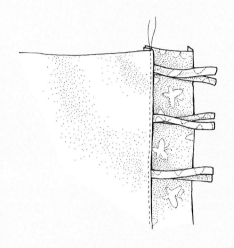

G. Spread open the top of the curtain, with the seams of both fabrics turned toward the curtain, and topstitch.

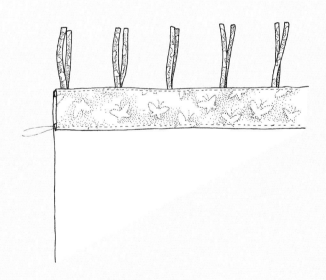

H. Topstitch the long edge hem of the top trim band to the curtain.

I. To hang the curtain, tie it over a curtain rod.

Fold-Up Shade

Like commercial blinds, this shade can be folded up and secured to let in light, or unfastened to hang down to the window sill, giving your bathroom complete privacy. Unlike commercial blinds, however, this one is made to your own specifications and in your own choice of fabrics, so it is highly personal as well as functional. The shade contains two pockets—one at the top and one at the bottom—which hold the curtain rod and a dowel or a second rod to weight the hem. The tabs which hold the shade when folded up are made of ribbon, and feature hook-and-loop fasteners sewn directly on the ribbon. Oversized fabric-covered buttons disguise the fasteners. When the shade is down, the ribbon tabs hang free. When the shade is folded up, the hook-and-loop fasteners keep the ribbon tabs tucked out of sight.

———

As the shade is folded up, the hook dots under the buttons will align with the loop dots on the back of the ribbon tab, so the ribbon tab is tucked out of sight.

MATERIALS

- L* + 4½in (L + 11.2cm) of 36 to 45in (90 to 112.5cm)-wide large woven check fabric A
- L* + 4½in (L + 11.2cm) of 36 to 45in (90 to 112.5cm)-wide small woven check fabric B
- 2(L* + 4½in) (L + 11.2cm) of 36 to 45in (90 to 112.5cm)-wide firm, washable, white fusible interfacing
- 4L* + 1in (2.5cm) of 1½in (4cm)-wide washable grosgrain ribbon to match color and check size of fabric B
- Six ⅞in (2.2cm) "cover your own" buttons
- Six ½in (1.2cm) sew-on hook-and-loop fastener dots
- 8in by ½in (20cm by 1.2cm) Velcro loop strip
- 1½ x ½in (4 x 1.2cm) Velcro hook strip
- Spring pressure rod to fit width of window (see step 1)
- Rod or dowel for bottom of shade, cut to equal width of window (see step 1)

*L = length (see step 1)

YOU'LL ALSO NEED:

Cutting shears or rotary cutter and board; marking pencil; tape measure; yardstick or right-angled ruler; double-sided fabric tape; sewing machine; thread to match fabric and ribbon; straight pins; iron and ironing board.

Instructions

1. Measure window. Measure width of window, just inside molded window frame (W). Measure height from top of inside molded window frame to sill (L).

2. Cut fabric. Cut straight line across grain following checks of both ginghams and weave of interfacing to ensure all fabrics are straight across grain. On flat surface, position both layers of interfacing with check fabrics on top, lining up each fabric evenly across grain and along selvages. Pin all four fabric layers together (see illustration A, facing page). Measure across grain W plus 1in (2.5cm) for seam allowance and mark on fabric, making sure that check designs will be centered on window. Measure down selvage length of shade (L) and add 3¾in (8.7cm) for hems, to allow 1¼in (3.1cm) hem with ½in (1.2cm) for seam allowance at top, and 1½in (3.7cm) hem with ½in (1.2cm) for seam allowance at bottom. (Total length is L + 3¾in [8.7cm]). Cut along checks to keep all grains even.

3. Sew fold-up shade. Use iron to fuse one rectangle of interfacing to wrong side of each checked fabric. With right sides facing, stitch all around shade through all four layers of fabric, ½in (1.2cm) from edge. Leave 9in (23cm) space for turning along center top (illustration B). Trim corners, then turn shade right side out. Press all edges including seam allowance of opening. Slipstitch closed.

4. Make ribbon tabs. Cut two lengths grosgrain ribbon measuring 2L + ½in (1.2cm). Fold each strip in half. Press raw edges ¼in (6mm) under at ends of each ribbon. Cut thin strip of hook tape measuring ¼ x 1½in (6mm x 4cm). Stitch in place on fold-under at one end of each ribbon (illustration C, detail). The side of the ribbon with the hook tape will become the front of the ribbon tab. Once the shade is hung, this side of the ribbon tab, with buttons covering the stitching, will face the interior of the room as shown in the photo above.

5. Add fasteners to tabs. Divide each half of ribbon tab into four equal parts from crease to fold under. Pin each marked spot. Center one hook dot over three pins, remove pin, and stitch into place on back side of tab (illustration C). Cut loop strip in half then stitch one half of loop strip at top of ribbon tab on rear side, beginning at center crease and continuing toward fold-under for four inches. Attach three loop dots as shown in illustration C on rear side of ribbon tab.

6. Press up hems. Measure 1¾in (4.3cm) for hem along top of shade, and press toward fabric B side (illustration D). Measure 2in (5cm) for hem along bottom of shade and press toward fabric B side.

7. Sew on tabs. Position and pin ribbon tabs on shade as shown in illustration E. Stitch in place with hourglass shape.

Secure free ends of ribbon lengths inside hem at bottom of Fabric B side of shade with double-stick tape, taking care to line grosgrain ribbon up with small checks.

8. Stitch hems and finish shade. Load machine with thread to match fabric A. Topstitch hems, catching and anchoring ribbon lengths on Fabric B side only (illustration E). To finish shade, cover button molds with fabric A, centering on large colored check. Hand-sew buttons over hook dots on ribbon tabs. Slip rod into top hem and rod or dowel into bottom hem. Hang shade at top of window just below window frame; spring pressure rod will automatically adjust to width.

Making the Roll-Up Shade

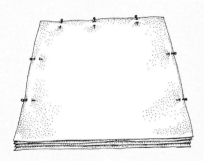

A. Line up two layers of fabric and two layers of interfacing, then pin together.

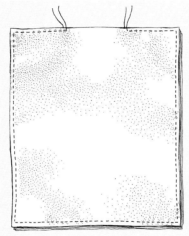

B. Stitch through all four layers of fabric, leaving an opening for turning at one edge.

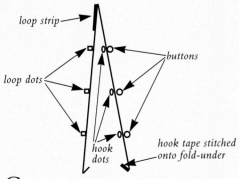

C. Attach the hook tape, the loop strip, and the loop and hook dots to the tab.

D. Measure and press hems at the top and bottom of the shade.

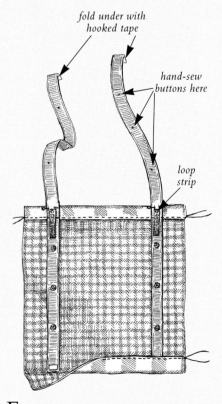

E. Attach the tabs to the curtain using an hourglass shape. Topstitch the hems, catching and anchoring the ribbon at the same time.

Picket-Style Window Valance

A valance adds a decorative finish to any bathroom, while also hiding the tops of your window blinds. The bold stripe used on this valance conveys a cheerful feel, and aids in creating the picket effect, which is determined by the width of the stripes. The wider the stripe, the fewer the picket points to sew. This finished valance measures 40in (1m) wide and 9in (23cm) deep from the bottom of the rod pocket to the end of the picket points. If you purchase fabric that measures 45in (112.5cm) wide, you will need to add extra material at both sides to create enough width. When adding the material, be sure to match the stripe or pattern appropriately.

—

For variation on this design, hang tassels or beads from the pickets.

MATERIALS

- **Sufficient wide stripe fabric to create a strip 13in (32.5cm) high by measurement of curtain rod when installed (bracket-to-bracket)**
- **Lining, same as for stripe fabric**
- **Sufficient 54in (135cm) wide interfacing to back stripe fabric**
- **Curtain or valance rod and brackets to fit your window**

YOU'LL ALSO NEED:

Yardstick; right-angled ruler; tape measure; sewing shears or rotary cutter and board; marking pencil; sewing machine; matching thread; straight pins; iron and ironing board; and knitting needle or chopstick to poke out picket points.

Instructions

1. Measure width of valance. Install rod at desired position. Measure installed rod including returns from bracket to bracket to obtain finished width of valance.

2. Prepare and cut fabric. To establish exact cross grain, cut across fabric at right angle to selvage. Cut away selvages. Press fabric. Lay fabric on flat surface, wrong side up. Mark then cut one or more strips of stripe fabric so it will equal the finished valance width measurement plus 1in (2.5cm) (for ½in [1.2cm] side seams) by 12¾in (31.8cm) depth (height). If more than one piece is required to obtain valance finished width, (as we have shown in the illustrations) plan strip placement to allow for matching design at each end of center piece and for ½in (1.2cm) seams where joined. Sew seams, if piecing is required, and press those seam allowances towards darker stripe to avoid show-through (illustration B).

3. Cut interfacing and lining. Using stripe valance panel as a pattern, cut out interfacing and lining pieces to same size. Lay lining right side up on interfacing, then position striped fabric face down on top. Pin all three together (illustration C).

4. Mark picket points. With marking pencil and right-angled ruler, mark points evenly all across bottom edges of fabric, using stripes as guide (illustration D). Keep points at right angles, as acute angles will be difficult to turn. Pin points and around edges through all three fabrics; leave 12in (30cm) opening at center top for turning (illustration E.).

5. Sew picket points and sides. Sew all around valance, pivoting machine needle at points, allowing ¼in (6mm) seams on points, and ½in (1.2cm) seams along sides and top. Trim away bottom of points and clip into each angle at top of point (illustration F). Clip all four corners at sides.

6. Finish valance. Turn valance right side out through opening. Gently poke out each point, then press points. Press edges of turning opening inwards. To create pocket for rod, press 1½in (4cm) hem towards wrong side along top edge, then topstitch, catching pressed opening in stitching (illustration G). Insert rod into hem and hang curtain (illustration H).

Making the Valance

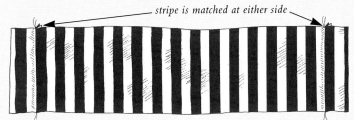

stripe is matched at either side

A. If piece is required to obtain width, stitch together three pieces of striped fabric.

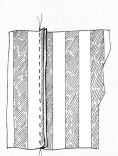

B. Press both seams towards the darker stripe to avoid show-through.

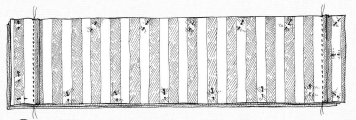

C. Lay down the interfacing, followed by the lining, right side up, and the striped fabric, right side down. Pin all three fabrics together.

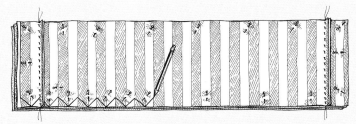

D. Mark and pin right-angled points across the bottom edge of the fabric, using the stripes as a guide.

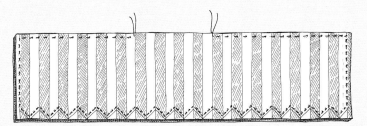

E. Sew around the valance, pivoting the machine needle at the points and leaving a 12in (30cm) opening for turning along the top edge.

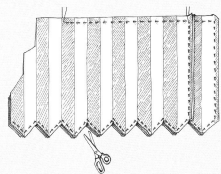

F. Trim the points, clip into each angle at the top of the points, and clip all four corners.

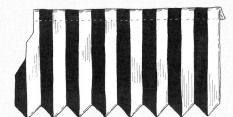

G. Turn the valance right side out through the opening, poke out and press the points, then press a hem along the top edge.

H. To hang the valance, insert the curtain rod through the pocket.

Tie-Tab Curtain

This gingham check tie-tab curtain is designed to cover the lower half of a bathroom window. The top half of the curtain has a wide border of sheer, translucent fabric to let in light, while the lower half of the curtain uses a gingham check fabric for privacy. The tabs, made from the same gingham fabric, tie over a curtain rod. As a finishing effect, add decorative buttons where the two fabrics are sewn together. This finished curtain measures about 9in (23cm) in depth for the sheer fabric section and 12in (30cm) in depth for the gingham. It's easy to adapt the instructions to your window size, however, and lengthen or shorten either section as you like.

For variation on this design, the top half of the curtain can be sewn from eyelet and the lower half from a country cotton print.

MATERIALS

- **About 1¼yd (115cm) 60in (150cm)-wide 1in (2.5cm) gingham check fabric**

  or

  1½yd (135cm) 45in (112.5cm)-wide 1in (2.5cm) gingham check fabric
- **18in (45cm) 60in (150cm)-wide washable translucent fabric**
- **Eight 1in (2.5cm)-diameter buttons**
- **Curtain rod and hardware**

YOU'LL ALSO NEED:

Cutting shears or rotary cutter and board; sewing machine; matching thread; marking pencil; tape measure; yardstick or right-angled ruler; straight pins; iron and ironing board; and chopstick for turning tabs.

Instructions

1. Measure window and prepare gingham fabric. Decide placement of curtain, then measure length and width of window. Double window width measurement to allow for fullness. Press gingham fabric. Cut along check from selvage to selvage to establish straight line. Lay gingham on flat surface.

2. Cut body of curtain. Use solid color check as guide for determining edges of side, top, and bottom hems. Allow 3½in (8.7cm) at top and bottom of curtain for hems. Allow 2in (5cm) at side hem. Determine placement of buttons on curtain body and placement of tabs on sheer fabric; tabs and buttons must align. Use crossed pins to mark button placement (see illustration A, facing page).

3. Cut and make tie tabs. Using solid color 1in (2.5cm) check for width of tab, cut eight strips measuring 24 x 3in (60 x 7.5cm), placing solid check in exact center of strip (illustration B). Tabs can be cut across grain to save yardage. Fold each strip in

> ## DESIGNER'S TIP
> **This curtain will work well with any two contrasting fabrics. They can both be sheer for windows that require less privacy; use two patterned fabrics for windows that require more privacy.**

Making the Tie-Tab Curtain

A. **Mark the button placement with crossed pins, and pin the hems all around.**

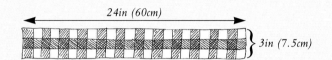

24in (60cm)

3in (7.5cm)

B. **Cut 8 tab strips with the solid check in the exact center.**

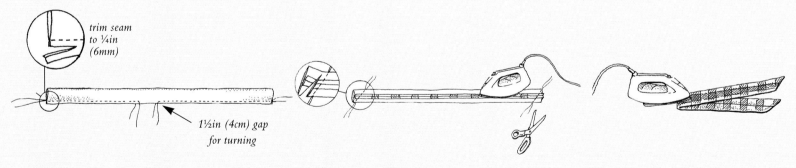

trim seam to ¼in (6mm)

1½in (4cm) gap for turning

C. **Fold the right sides together, then stitch, leaving a gap for turning. Trim the seam to ¼in (6mm).**

D. **Roll seam to top and press the seam open, then stitch and trim a slanting line across both ends.**

E. **Press each finished tab in half, seamline facing. The crease will be used to indicate the stitching line when the ties are sewn to the sheer fabric.**

This curtain design will also work well with lace and solid-colored fabric.

half lengthwise, right sides together. Stitch along raw edges using ⅜in (9.5mm) seam allowance. Leave 1½in (4cm) gap in middle for turning (illustration C). Trim seam to ¼in (6mm). Roll seam-line so it is centered on top. Press seam open. Sew and trim slant-ing line across both ends (illustration D). Use chopstick to turn right side out through gap. Press to evenly line up gingham check design. Fold each finished tab in half, seamlines together, and press crease (illustration E).

4. Cut translucent fabric. Press translucent fabric. Pull thread across from selvage to selvage to establish exact cross grain. Mark and cut rectangle measuring 15½in (38.7cm) by width of ging-ham. Press ½in (12mm) fold at bottom hem toward right side, then stitch (illustration F). Press up again and fold 3in (7.5cm) from stitching but do not sew. For top hem, fold upper edge down ½in (12mm) to wrong side and press. Then fold down to right side 3½in (8.7cm) and press. This crease will serve as a guiding line in step 5.

5. Sew tabs to sheer fabric. Lay translucent fabric flat, right side up, then open 3in (7.5cm) top hem. Pin center crease of each tab along pressed-in crease of top, spacing tabs to match pinned button positions on gingham. Sew tabs in place (illustra-tion G), through crease line, then back-stitch to secure. Fold side hems 1in (2.5cm) to wrong side, then fold again, pin, and stitch. Press top hem and ½in (12mm) fold-under to wrong side then

stitch 3in (7.5cm) top hem on wrong side of translucent fabric.

6. Sew gingham curtain. Press 1in (2.5cm) double side hems in gingham. Pin, then sew side hems from right side so stitch line runs along exact edge of check. Press, then stitch bottom 3in (7.5cm) hem with ¼in (6mm) turn-in (illustration H). Press ¼in (6mm) then 3in (7.5cm) hem at top edge of curtain.

7. Join fabrics and finish. Lay top of gingham curtain over bottom hem of sheer fabric, overlapping 3in (7.5cm) (illustration I). Pin in place, then stitch lower edge of top gingham hem from right side through all layers of fabric to bottom fold of sheer top hem, catching both curtain pieces together. Remove crease in sheer fabric by pressing. To finish, sew buttons in place, catching both fabrics. Press curtain. Hang on curtain rod by tying tabs into bows (illustration J).

Finishing the Tie-Tab Curtain

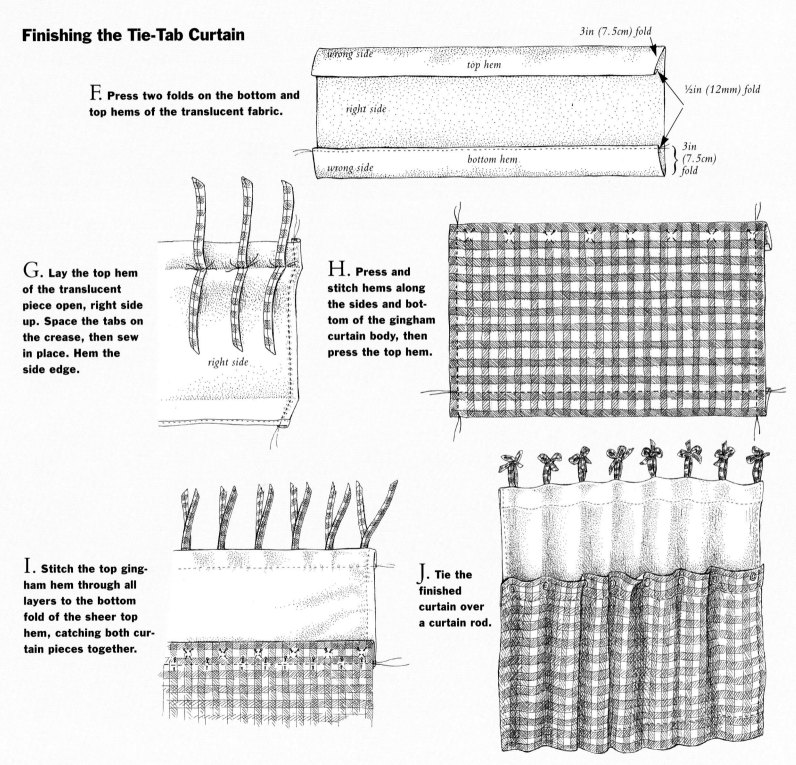

F. **Press two folds on the bottom and top hems of the translucent fabric.**

3in (7.5cm) fold

wrong side

top hem

right side

½in (12mm) fold

wrong side

bottom hem

3in (7.5cm) fold

G. **Lay the top hem of the translucent piece open, right side up. Space the tabs on the crease, then sew in place. Hem the side edge.**

right side

H. **Press and stitch hems along the sides and bottom of the gingham curtain body, then press the top hem.**

I. **Stitch the top gingham hem through all layers to the bottom fold of the sheer top hem, catching both curtain pieces together.**

J. **Tie the finished curtain over a curtain rod.**

85

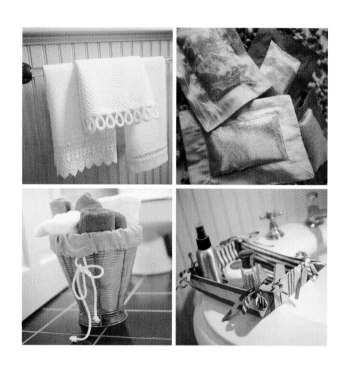

shelf and counter

Accented Guest Towels

Looking for a way to dress up your powder room? Consider these decorative guest towels, designed to dress up an ordinary towel rack. Start with plain linen or cotton guest towels, then add decorative accents such as silk flower petals, silk cord, beads, or shirt buttons.

——

Towels shown, clockwise left to right: Petals and pearls towel, silk rose towel, silk cord and beads towel, and shirt buttons and running stitch towel.

MATERIALS

■ **Cotton or linen hand towels**

Petals and pearls towel:

■ **27 ³⁄₈in (1cm) to ³⁄₄in (1.8cm)-diameter flower petals**

■ **27 ³⁄₁₆in (4.8mm)-diameter seed pearls**

Silk rose towel:

■ **Silk rose**

Silk cord and beads towel:

■ **1yd (90cm) ³⁄₁₆in (4.8mm)-wide silk cord**

■ **6 ³⁄₈in (1cm)-diameter glass beads**

■ **6 ¹⁄₄in (6mm)-diameter glass beads**

■ **Embroidery floss**

Shirt buttons and running stitch towel:

■ **15 white shirt buttons**

■ **Embroidery floss**

YOU'LL ALSO NEED:

Sewing shears; ruler; pins; beading needle; matching threads; sewing machine with (optional) zigzag; and monofilament thread.

Instructions

Petals and pearls towel:

1. Prepare and place flowers. Remove blossoms from small silk flowers by separating blossoms from stamen. Scatter blossoms randomly along one edge of towel, then pin each blossom in place.

2. Sew flowers. Hand-tack each blossom to towel, finishing each with seed pearl in center (see illustration A, facing page).

Silk rose towel:

1. Sew rose on towel. Hand-tack rose in place on towel.

Silk cord and beads towel:

1. Arrange and sew silk cord. Place loops and curves of silk cord across one hem of towel, then secure with pins (illustration B). Hand-sew silk cord in place, or sew a widely spaced zigzag using contrasting thread (illustration C).

2. Add beads. Hand-sew beads in place with embroidery floss. Position beads under silk cord to form tassel effect.

Shirt buttons and running stitch towel:

1. Running stitch. Using sewing needle and embroidery floss, begin running stitch with knot and ³⁄₈in (1cm) end of thread showing on right side (illustration D). Sew even running stitches ³⁄₈in (1cm) long across one end of towel ½in (12mm) above decorative hem line.

2. Sew buttons. Arrange three-button groups along one hem of towel, then hand-sew each in place (illustration E).

DESIGNER'S TIPS

For a holiday variation on this design, use red flower petals and white pearls on pine-green towels. For an elegant, sculptural look, combine white towels with white trim elements.

Making the Accented Guest Towels

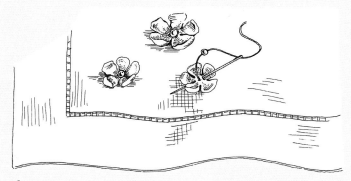

A. Hand-tack each blossom to the towel, finishing each with a small seed pearl.

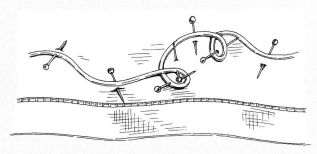

B. Place loops and curves of cord across one hem of the towel, then secure by pinning through cords.

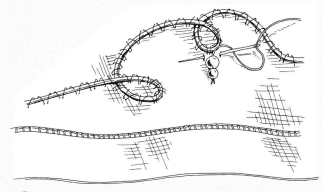

C. Hand-sew the cord in place, or machine-sew a widely spaced zigzag using contrasting thread.

D. Start the running stitch with a knot, letting the end of the thread show on the right side.

E. Arrange three-button groups along one hem of the towel, then hand-sew them in place.

Silk-and-Organza Sachets

These elegant sachets, filled with fragrant materials such as fir needles, dried roses, dried lavender, and citrus peel, are sewn from two types of fabric: silk dupioni for the outer flanged edging, and gold metallic organza for the interior portion. The delicate mesh of the organza lets the scent of the sachet's contents escape. Although most of these potpourri ingredients are fragrant on their own, the scent can be enhanced by adding a fixative ingredient and an essential oil or fragrance oil. The fixative retains the scent from the oils and keeps the potpourri fragrant for a longer period of time.

—

The fabric colors used for these sachets coordinate with the contents: moss green for fir needles, orange yellow for dried citrus peels, soft purple for dried lavender, and magenta for dried rose petals.

MATERIALS

Yields four sachets

- **1-2 cups (454g-909g) dried lavender, rose petals, balsam fir needles, cedar chips or citrus peels**
- **¼ cup (56.8g) oak moss or cellulose fiber**
- **Essential oil to match potpourri**
- **9in (23cm) 45in (112.5cm)-wide fabric or remnants**
- **4½in (11.2cm) 45in (112.5cm)-wide gold metallic organza or other meshlike fabric**
- **Thread to match fabrics**

YOU'LL ALSO NEED:

Sewing machine; rotary cutter; transparent gridded ruler; self-healing cutting mat; iron; fabric chalk pencil; sewing shears; hand-sewing needle; pins; knitting needle; and quart-size plastic bag.

Instructions

1. Mix potpourri. If using oak moss, cut or tear it into ½in (1.2cm) pieces. Place moss or fiber in plastic bag, add 10 drops essential oil, seal bag, and shake well. Add dried material and shake. Set sealed bag aside in dark place for two to three weeks.

2. Cut fabric pieces. Using rotary cutter, grid ruler, and cutting mat, cut four 7⅞ x 9⅝in (17.7 x 24.6cm) sachet covers and four 3⅝ x 5¼in (9.1 x 13cm) pillow backings from silk; longer edge should run along crosswise grain. Cut four 3⅝ x 5¼in (9.1x 13cm) organza pillow fronts.

3. Crease cover to mark flange. Using matching thread, staystitch silk sachet cover scant ¼in (6mm) from edge all around. Lay cover flat, right side up. Using chalk, mark a dot 1⅜in (3.4cm) from each corner. Draw a line connecting dots adjacent to same corner. Fold each corner diagonally on chalk line until creases match, then press toward wrong side to set crease. Lay cover flat, right side up, and finger-press (see illustration A, facing page). Repeat process for each cover.

4. Sew flange. Press raw edges ¼in (6mm) toward wrong side, just beyond stitching line. Lay cover right side up. Fold corner in half diagonally, aligning raw edges, and pin. Crease flange allowance, but do not crease body of cover. Stitch from fold to staystitching, following diagonal crease set in step 3 and backtacking at beginning and end (illustration B). Repeat to sew remaining corners. Trim excess fabric ¼in (6mm) beyond stitching. Press seam allowances open. Turn cover right side out, push out corners with point turner, and tuck raw edges to inside. Press well (illustration C). Repeat process for each cover.

5. Sew and fill pillow insert. Fold silk pillow backing in half lengthwise, right sides together. Starting and ending 1in (2.5cm) from raw edge, at the fold, stitch ⅛in (3mm) dart ending 1in (2.5cm) from opposite raw edge (illustration D). Open flat, wrong side up, and press dart to one side. Turn pillow backing over. Set organza pillow front right side up on top of it, raw edges matching. Stitch on three sides scant ¼in (6mm) from edge to make pocket. Put ¼ cup to ½ cup (56.8g to 113.6g) potpourri into pocket until about one-third full (illustration E). Pin open end, then test-fit pocket under flange. Flange should fit snugly, concealing raw edges and stitching. Stitch pocket closed to make pillow. Repeat process for each insert.

6. Assemble sachet. Center pillow insert under flange, as in step 5. Pin through all layers. Topstitch flange edge around all four sides (illustration F). Press flange.

Making the Sachets

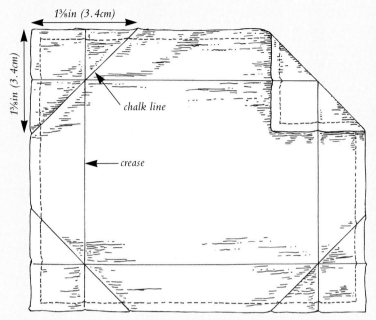

1⅜in (3.4cm)

1⅜in (3.4cm)

chalk line

crease

A. **Crease a silk rectangle to mark the flange edge.**

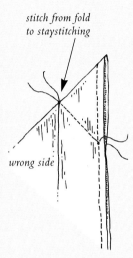

stitch from fold
to staystitching

wrong side

B. **Sew the corners diagonally to set the flange.**

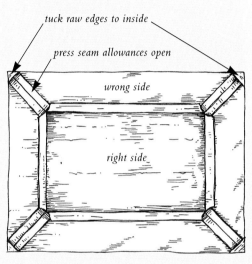

tuck raw edges to inside

press seam allowances open

wrong side

right side

C. **Trim excess fabric ¼in (6mm) beyond stitching, then press seam allowances open.**

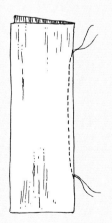

D. **Fold the silk pillow backing in half, then stitch a dart along the fold line.**

E. **Set the organza pillow front on top and stitch on three sides to make a pocket. Fill with potpourri until about one-third full.**

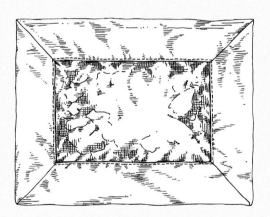

F. **Trap the insert edges under the flange and topstitch in place.**

Lace-Edged Hand Towels

These crisp, white, lace-touched hand towels may look hand embroidered, but they're actually easy to make. Start by purchasing white piqué, available in many weights and fabric variations, from fine pinwales to fancy jacquards. The finished towels here measure 13½ x 25in (33.7 x 62.5cm), so you can get three towels from ¾yd (67.5cm) of 45in (112.5cm)-wide piqué, or four towels from ¾yd (67.5 cm) of 60in (150cm)-wide fabric. Towels shown, left to right: Filigree lace-edged towel, looped laced-edge towel, and cut-out laced-edge towel.

—

You can use just about any lace motif you want for the trimming, but be sure it is washable. The trims can be applied to one or to both ends of the towels.

MATERIALS

- **¾yd (67.5cm) 45in (112.5cm)-wide piqué (yields three towels)**

  or

  ¾yd (67.5cm) 60in (150cm)-wide piqué (yields four towels)
- **½yd (45cm) to 3yd (2.7m) lace trim as needed**

YOU'LL ALSO NEED:

Tape measure or ruler; marking pencil; sewing shears; sewing machine (optional) with zigzag stitch; matching thread; and safety pin.

SEWING TIPS

Do not stretch lace because it shrinks in the wash. To avoid wrinkling, stretch piqué underneath the lace as you sew.

If using very intricate lace, snip between the motifs and separate them in order to place the design as if it was custom-made. Small pieces of vintage lace or embroidery can be sewn onto towels as appliqués.

Instructions

Cut-out lace-edged towel:

1. Preparation. Establish straight grain across fabric by pulling thread from selvage to selvage. Cut fabric into pieces measuring 15 x 27in (37.5 x 67.5cm). If you apply trim at only one end, finish other end with a simple topstitched hem.

2. Determine best side of lace. Lace used for this towel has an imitation hemstitched effect made of tiny crossed ribbons that are held in place on each side with ¼in (6mm) headings, which will be hidden.

3. Create lace hem. From piqué, measure and cut 4 x 15in (10 x 37.5cm) strip. Trim lace to 14in (35 cm), then position on edge of fabric strip with ½in (1.2cm) extra fabric at each end; fabric will be hemmed to match length of lace later on. Sew lace to piqué strip, right sides facing, using ¼in (6mm) seams (see illustration A, facing page). Fold piqué strip lengthwise with right sides facing, trapping lace. Sew ¼in (6mm) seam following previous seam stitches to form tube with lace trapped inside. Trim off corners at each end (illustration B). Use large safety pin to turn tube right side out (illustration C) and press. Poke in ½in (1.2cm) seams at each end and press (illustration D), making sure the pushed-in hem will line up with the side hems. Topstitch ¼in (6mm) across piqué seam to hold lace firm and flat.

4. Attach lace length to towel. Lay free side of lace on raw

Making the Lace-Edged Towels

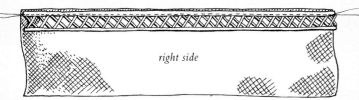

A. Sew the insertion lace to the strip, right sides facing.

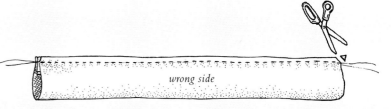

B. Fold the piqué strips with the lace trapped inside, then sew to form a tube. Trim off the corners.

C. Using a large safety pin, turn the tube right side out, then press.

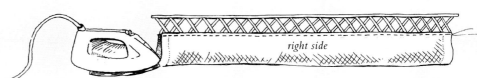

D. Poke in the seams at either end and press. Topstitch across the piqué seam.

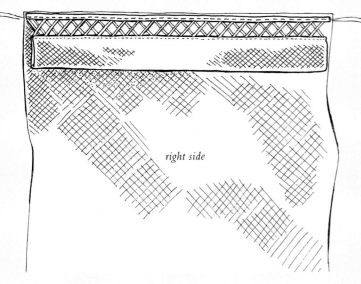

E. Sew the free side of the lace to the raw end of the towel.

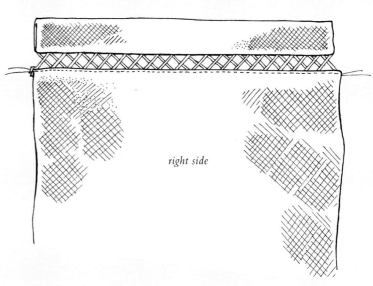

F. Press the seam away from the insertion lace and topstitch on the piqué.

Towels (left to right): Filigree lace, looped lace, and cut-out lace edge.

end of towel body, right sides together. Sew lace edge to towel using ¼in (6mm) seams (illustration E). Press seam away from lace. Topstitch ¼in (6mm) on piqué to hold lace flat and to cover raw edge of piqué (illustration F).

5. Finish side seams. Press ¼in (6mm) hem to wrong side twice along both sides of towel body. Line up pushed-in hem of strip with side hems. Slip-stitch hems on strip hem, then machine-stitch side hems (illustration G).

Filigree lace-edged towel:

1. Preparation. Establish straight grain across fabric by pulling thread from selvage to selvage. Cut fabric into pieces measuring 15 x 27in (37.5 x 67.5cm). If you apply trim at only one end, finish other end with a simple topstitched hem.

2. Establish dimensions. Measure length of lace border, then trim lace border to match towel width or visa versa. Determine right side of lace, then center lace across towel.

3. Prepare end hems. Press ¼in (6mm) single hem toward right side at one end.

4. Attach lace border. Sew lace to right side of piqué, covering pressed hem as you go. Add topstitch at edge of hem to stabilize lace and hem (illustration H). Repeat at other end of towel, or finish end to match sides.

5. Sew side hems. Press ¼in (6mm) hem twice on both sides. Topstitch side hems, trapping lace as you stitch (illustration I).

Looped lace-edged towel:

1. Preparation. Establish straight grain across fabric by pulling thread from selvage to selvage. Cut fabric into pieces measuring 15 x 27in (37.5 x 67.5cm). If you apply trim at only one end, finish other end with a simple topstitched hem.

2. Hem piqué. Press ¼in (6mm) hem twice to wrong side all around piqué towel. Topstitch hem.

3. Apply lace. Establish right side of lace. Pin in place along one edge of piqué towel. Sew on using straight line (if lace permits), covering as much of hem as possible (illustration J). Do not stretch lace. If necessary, stitch lace using zigzag stitch and monofilament thread.

Finishing the Lace-Edged Towels

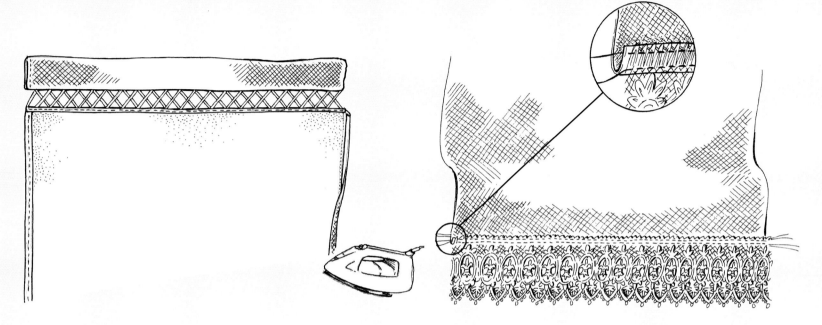

G. **Press the hems along both sides and stitch.**

H. **Sew the lace to the right side of the piqué.**

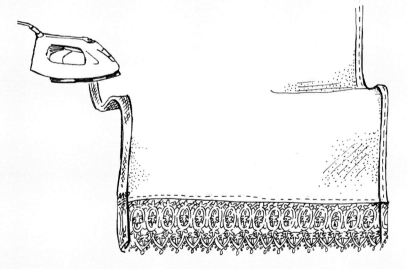

I. **Add topstitching along the side hems.**

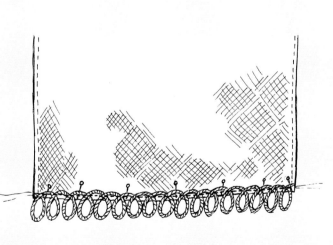

J. **Stitch the lace in place using a straight line if possible.**

Lined Wire Basket

This modern wire basket features a removable fabric liner which fits snugly inside the basket. The liner extends over the top of the basket and is held in place by a drawstring tie. To ensure a good fit, the liner is tube-shaped, with the tube pleated to a circle at the bottom of the basket. Because you can see through the basket from the outside, you'll need to finish the seams neatly on both sides, which is why the liner is made with flat-fell (shirt) seams. For the same reason, choose fabric that looks good on both sides, such as plain or fancy woven cotton or linen.

———

The instructions here can be adapted to any size or type of waste basket, although you will need to adjust the bottom, height, and circumference to fit the basket.

MATERIALS

- **½yd (45cm) 54in (135cm)-wide fabric**

  or

  ¾yd (67.5cm) 45in (112.5cm)-wide fabric
- **Wastebasket**

YOU'LL ALSO NEED:

Sewing machine preferably with zigzag capability, or if using straight stitch machine, finish edges with pinking shears or bias binding; sewing shears; marking pencil; ruler; tape measure; compass or small plate to mark circle; matching thread; iron and ironing board; and safety pin.

Instructions

1. Prepare fabric and measure basket. Press fabric. Straighten grain from selvage to selvage by pulling a cross-thread. Measure height of inner basket plus 5in (12.5cm) to allow for seams and fold-over hem at top. Measure circumference of basket top. Add 4in (10cm) for ½in (1.2cm) seams and for extra ease to help slip liner on and off. Measure diameter of inner bottom of basket (illustration A, facing page). Record measurements.

2. Cut pieces. On fabric, mark rectangle with measurements noted above, and cut out. Mark and cut circle same size as bottom of basket plus ½in (1.2cm) for seams all around. For ties, cut piece measuring 2 x 45in (5 x 112.5cm). If using fabric narrower than 50in (125cm), cut tie in two pieces as seam will be hidden in casing (illustration B).

3. Prepare pieces for sewing. On one short side of body liner (side seam A) make ¼in (6mm) notch approximately 1¾in (4.3cm) down, then make a second notch 1¼in (3.1cm) beyond first notch. On second short side of body liner (side seam B), make ½in (1.2cm) deep notch 3in (7.5cm) down (illustration C). These notches indicate casing opening on side seam into which tie will be inserted. Fold bottom circle in half and then in quarters, then make notches at folds to divide circumference into even eighths (illustration D).

4. Press and stitch seam allowances. On side seam A of body liner, press ¼in (6mm) seam allowance from top edge down side to 3in (7.5cm) notch. On side B press ½in (1.2cm) seam allowance from top to notch. To form liner tube with shirt seam, position side seams A and B together, "right sides" facing. Do not line up raw edges, but instead take ¼in (6mm) seam allowance on side A and ½in (1.2cm) seam allowance on side B. Sew seam from top of rectangle, going only to first notch on side A. Press seam open above 3in (7.5cm) notches but do not sew (illustration E). Continue sewing A side to B side from 3in (7.5cm) notches downwards using same seam allowances as above. Press seam with both seam allowances to one side so that wider seam allowance covers smaller seam allowance (illustration E). Fold

Making the Lined Wire Basket

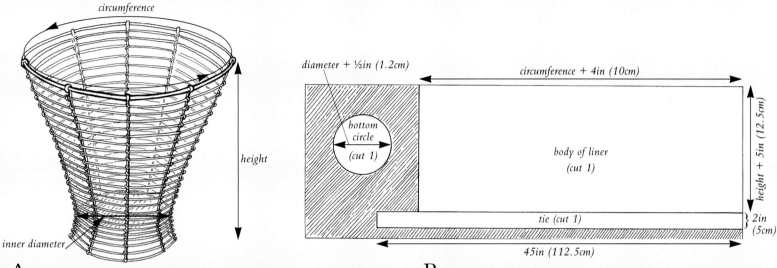

A. **Measure your basket: circumference of top opening, height, and inner diameter of bottom circle.**

B. **Use the measurements to cut a body liner rectangle, bottom circle, and tie.**

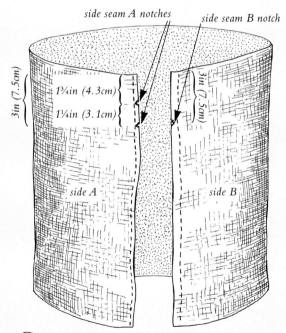

C. **Notch the liner to locate tie opening in the seam, and allowances for the shirt seam.**

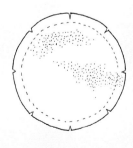

D. **Divide the bottom circle into eighths and notch.**

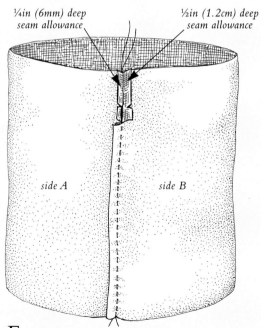

E. **Press and sew seams, leaving the opening for the tie. Press to one side so the wider seam allowance covers the smaller one.**

105

Solid cottons that look equally good on both sides, such as broadcloth, poplin or muslin, would be a good choice for this liner because they come in a wide range of colors. Try woven shirting stripes in oxford cloth, or reversible cotton damask.

¼in (6mm) of wider seam B over ¼in (6mm) of seam A to cover it. Edge-stitch on fold through all layers. On seam inside basket there will be a seam line and one stitch line showing (illustration F). On opposite side there will be two rows of stitches approximately ¼in (6mm) apart. Press seam.

5. Sew opening for tie and hem. Topstitch around opening (illustration G); pressed-open space in seam will measure 1¼in (3.1cm). This opening for tie will be on outside of basket when in place. To sew hem, press ½in (1.2cm) turning along top of liner, then 1¼in (3.1cm) for hem. Sew hem. Once hem is sewn, tie opening will be at top of liner (illustration H).

6. Attach bottom circle. Mark bottom of liner tube into eighths and notch (illustration I). Pin tube to circle, matching notches. Pleat excess fabric between notches, folding pleats in same direction (illustration J and detail). Sew circle to tube using ½in (1.2cm) seams (illustration J). Finish bottom seam using one of three methods: a) zigzag raw edges; b) sew seams together ¼in (6mm) from seam, then pink; or c) bind edges with bias tape.

7. Make tie. Press ¼in (6mm) hem all around tie piece. Press in half lengthwise, wrong sides together. Edge-stitch around tie. Press. Thread tie into liner opening using large safety pin. Place liner in basket, letting top fold over edge of basket (illustration K).

Finishing the Lined Wire Basket

seam outside basket

seam inside basket

F. **Fold wider seam over narrow seam to cover it, and edge-stitch through all layers on the fold.**

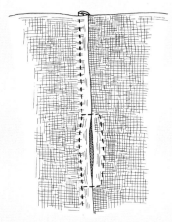

G. **Sew around the slot for the ties.**

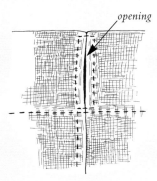

opening

H. **Sew the hem. After the hem is sewn, the tie opening will move to the top of the liner.**

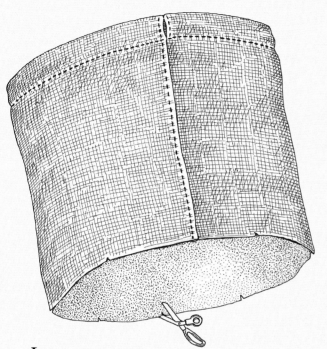

I. **Divide the body liner into eighths and notch for the pleats.**

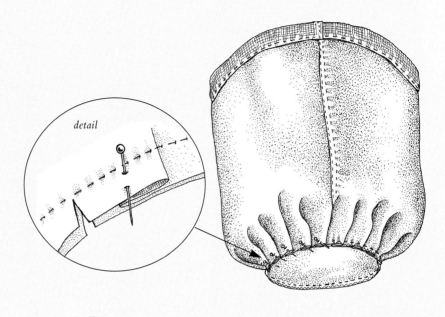

detail

J. **Pin the liner and the circle together, matching the notches, and sew.**

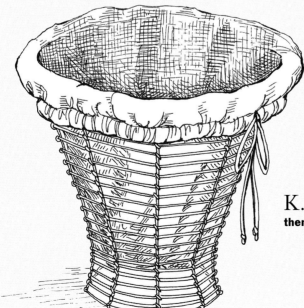

K. **Thread the tie into the opening, then place the liner in the basket.**

Fabric-Covered Bath Tray

This bath and vanity tray, designed to hold anything from makeup and perfume bottles to rolled washcloths, can be assembled from fabric remnants. To give the tray a firm base and sides, plastic needlepoint canvas is inserted along the edges and bottom. Once the ties are tied, the sides will stand upright. This tray can be custom fit to the objects it will hold. For a large version designed to hold rolled towels, for instance, simply measure the rolled towel and adjust the pattern as necessary. You could also make a long narrow tray to fit the back of a toilet, or a series of small trays to hold cotton balls, cotton swabs, and the like.

———

For variation on this design, make a plastic-lined tray for holding your sink soap.

MATERIALS

- 12 x 24in (30 x 60cm) fabric remnant (for outside of tray. Note: If ties are to be cut on bias, you will need 1yd (90cm) of fabric.)
- 12 x 14in (30 x 35cm) fabric remnant (for inside of tray)
- 8 x 14in (20.5 x 35cm) piece plastic needlepoint canvas

YOU'LL ALSO NEED:

Pattern (see page 121); access to photocopier with enlargement capabilities; ruler; marking pencil; straight pins or water soluble ink pen; sewing shears; sewing machine; matching thread; and sewing needle.

DESIGNER'S TIPS

For variation on this design, make the tray with black cotton on the exterior and white piqué lining, then fill the tray with red washcloths.

For a faster version of the tray, use ¼in (6mm)-wide red grosgrain ribbons for the ties.

Instructions

1. Make pattern. Prepare pattern found on page 121. Copy and enlarge pattern so grid blocks measure 1in (2.5cm) square.

2. Cut fabric. Mark and cut one pattern from each fabric. Make three tiny notches at edges of each fabric piece to mark tie placement. To make ties, cut eight strips measuring 10 x 1in (25.5 x 2.5cm) from larger piece of fabric. (If fabric is striped or plaid, cut strips on bias.)

3. Make ties. Press ¼in (6mm) hem on three sides of strips. Fold each tie in half lengthwise, wrong sides together, and press. Edge-stitch around the three hemmed sides. Ties should measure ¼ x 9¾in (6mm x 24.8cm) when finished.

4. Cut support pieces and determine placement. Cut plastic canvas as follows: two pieces measuring 5⅞ x 1⅞in (14.7 x 4.7cm) for short uprights; two pieces measuring 7⅞ x 1⅞in (19.7 x 4.7cm) for longer uprights; and one piece measuring 5⅞ x 7⅞in (14.7 x 19.7cm) for base. Using water-soluble pen or row of pins, mark sides of tray with stitching lines to aid in placement of ties.

5. Position ties. Place unsewn end of eight ties at notches on right side of inner fabric; place raw edges together so ties lie toward center of tray. Pin, then stitch in place (see illustration A, facing page).

6. Sew tray pieces together. Lay tray sections on top of each other, right sides facing. Sew pieces together using ¼in (6mm) seams; leave one end open for turning (illustration B). Clip curves. Turn right side out and press. Topstitch around all edges except opening.

7. Insert stiffening. Insert one short upright piece of canvas at end opposite opening. Stitch along marking lines to enclose canvas. Repeat for two longer upright pieces. Insert base piece and enclose with stitching. Finally, insert last short upright piece. Press in turnings at opening and slip-stitch opening closed (illustration C).

8. Finish tray. Topstitch all round top of tray. Tie bows at corners so sides stand upright (illustration D).

Making the Bath Tray

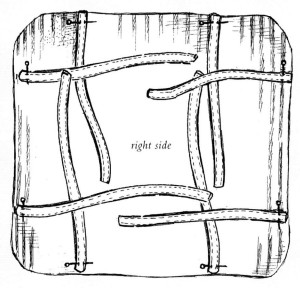

A. **Position the ties on the right side of the inner fabric, raw edges together. Pin, then stitch in place.**

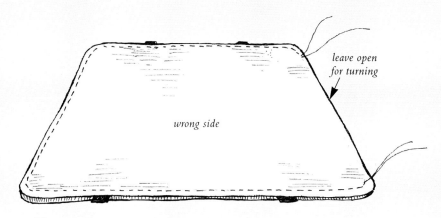

leave open for turning

wrong side

B. **With right sides facing, sew the two main sections together. Leave one end open for turning.**

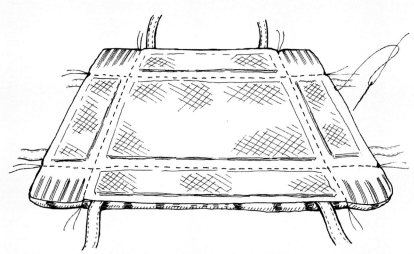

C. **Insert and stitch around the canvas pieces, then slip-stitch the opening closed.**

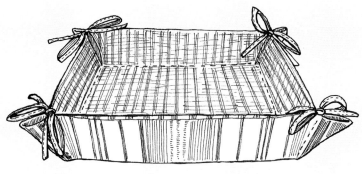

D. **Tie the bows at the corners so the sides stand upright.**

111

Pompon Wash Mitt

If you're looking for a way to recycle old bath towels, this quick and easy wash mitt may be the answer. One-quarter yard (23cm) of terry cloth (about one-half of a towel), is enough fabric to make three bath mitts. When selecting terry cloth for this project, look for good-quality, thick toweling. If your favorite color comes only in thin terry, double it up, then use it as if it were one piece of cloth. You'll also need washable trim and pompons, which can be found in various colors and sizes at craft and sewing shops. You can also make your own pompons using embroidery floss.

———

If you cannot find matching fringe and pompons, you can cut the pompons off cotton pompon edging. For variation on this design, sew on tiny ¼in (6mm) multicolored pompons so that they look like confetti.

MATERIALS

- ¼yd (23cm) 45in (112.5cm)-wide terry cloth
- 12 washable ¾in (18mm)-diameter pompons

  or

  16 washable ¼in (6mm)-diameter pompons

  or

  1yd (90cm) of cotton pompon fringe (cut off pompons before using)
- 15in (37.5cm) washable 1in (2.5cm)-wide fringe

YOU'LL ALSO NEED:

Pins; ruler; sewing shears; sewing machine preferably with zigzag capability; and matching thread.

Instructions

1. Cut terry cloth. With pins, mark two pieces of terry cloth measuring 7½ x 9in (18.7 x 23cm). Cut pieces (see illustration A, facing page) on flat surface.

2. Finish edges. To prevent edges of terry cloth from raveling, zigzag around all edges with matching thread (illustration B). If your machine does not have a zigzag capability, topstitch ¼in (6mm) hem around pieces.

3. Mark mitt for pompons. Spread terry pieces. With pins, mark locations for pompons, spacing them about 3in (7.5cm) apart (illustration C). Avoid placing pompons near edges.

4. Attach pompons. Place one pompon on mark. Spread pompon as flat as possible, pushing yarns away from its center. In center, make series of zig-zag stitches in place by machine, or stitch by hand. Fluff pompon to hide stitches (illustration D).

5. Sew mitt together. Place two mitt pieces right sides (with pompons) together. Stitch around three sides, leaving one short side open (illustration E). Turn right side out.

6. Attach fringe. To sew fringe opening of mitt, place fringe around mitt opening, with fringe facing towards mitt. Stitch along line where loose threads of fringe begin (illustration F). Fold fringe downwards, away from mitt, and topstitch ¼in (6mm) through both terry and fringe (illustration G).

Making the Pompon Wash Mitt

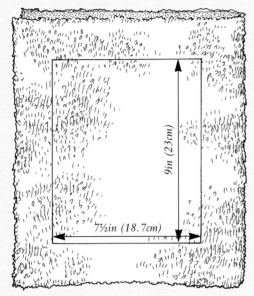

A. Mark and cut the terry cloth into two pieces.

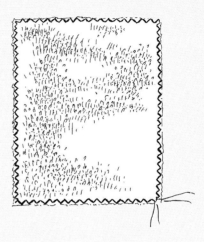

B. Finish the edges of the cut pieces.

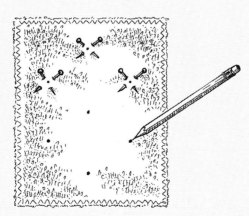

C. Mark the position of the pompons with pins.

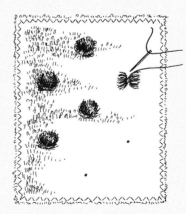

D. Spread the pompon apart, then stitch in place using a series of zig-zag or hand stitches.

For a special gift idea, place tiny bottles of bath gel in the mitt and tie it closed with a matching ribbon.

MAKING YOUR OWN POMPONS

You can make your own pompons using skeins of six-strand embroidery floss. Available in a wide array of colors, the floss fluffs out into full pompons with a soft chenille-like surface.

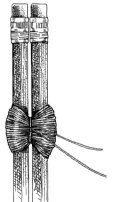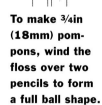

To make ¾in (18mm) pompons, wind the floss over two pencils to form a full ball shape.

Slide a 10in (25cm) long piece of floss between the pencils and knot tightly.

Clip through the loops on each side of the knot and fluff out the pompon. Clip the long ends.

Finishing the Pompon Wash Mitt

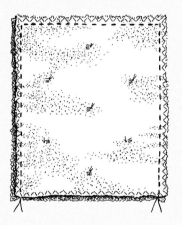

E. With right sides together, sew around three sides of the mitt, leaving one short side open. Turn the mitt right side out.

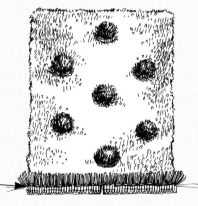

F. Place the cut end of the fringe facing toward the mitt and sew in place.

stitch line

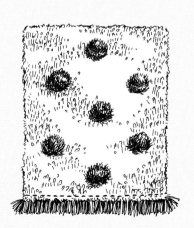

G. Finish the mitt by folding the fringe down and topstitching in place.

appendix

Glossary of Terms

Bias: Any diagonal that intersects the lengthwise or crosswise grain.

Button mold kit: Kit for making covered buttons. Includes a button shell, which is covered with fabric, and a button back, which holds the fabric in place over the shell.

Cutting shears: Scissors especially designed for cutting fabric or pattern, as angle of lower blade lets the fabric lie flat.

Edge-stitching: stitching as close as possible to the edge of a piece of fabric or trim.

Fabric glue stick: Fabric glue in a stick form, like lip balm.

Fabric marking pen or pencil: Designed for marking alterations. Available in different forms, including chalk wedges, chalk-in-pencil form, and pens whose ink washes or fades away with time.

Finger press: To press a fold or section of fabric using one's fingers instead of an iron. Usually reserved for small areas or areas where a crisp fold is not necessary.

Foot-space: Unit of measurement determined by the width of the sewing machine foot. On most machines, it measures approximately ¼in (6mm).

Grain: Most fabrics are made by weaving two or more threads at right angles to each other. Grain indicates the particular direction of the thread: lengthwise grain runs parallel to the selvage, while crosswise grain runs perpendicular to the selvage.

Hand baste: Hand basting (or tacking) is used to temporarily hold fabric together during construction.

Hand-sewing needle: A group of needles, most of them "sharp" needles, designed for general purpose sewing.

Hook-and-loop tape: A type of fastener featuring two tape strips, one with a looped nap and the other with a hooked nap. When pressed together, the surfaces grip and remain locked until pulled apart.

Machine back-stitch: When you start and stop sewing, make an extra stitch or two to hold the ends of the thread firmly and to prevent the stitches from opening. Lift the foot, shift the fabric, and add a stitch or two, or use the back stitch lever to go back one stitch, and then forward again.

Machine baste: Long, straight stitch used to hold fabric layers together during construction or permanent machine stitching.

Machine stitch: Using the sewing machine for a regular stitch length (10 to 15 stitches per inch [1.5 to 2.5mm]).

Muslin: Inexpensive cotton, made in a variety of weights, from gauzelike fabric to sheeting. Suitable for aprons, linings, shirts, and sheets.

Pinking shears: These special scissors cut a zigzag, fray resistant edge. Best used for finishing seams and unfinished edges on fabric.

Raw edges: Cut or unsewn edges of fabric.

Right side: The one side of fabric that features the pattern or color of the cloth.

Rotary cutter: A smaller version of the giant rotary cutters used by the garment industry, this cutting tool works like a pizza cutter and can be used by right- or left-handed sewers. Should be used with a self-healing cutting mat, which protects both the table and the blade.

Rough cut: Cutting fabric to a rough fit; leave about 2in (5cm) extra on larger projects; up to ¾in (1.8cm) extra on smaller projects. Designed to reduce the amount of fabric without requiring an exact pattern or template.

Running stitch: A very short, even stitch used for fine seaming, tucking, mending, gathering, and other such delicate sewing. Resembles basting, except stitches are smaller and usually permanent.

Seam ripper: Handheld device featuring a sharp, curved edge for opening stitched seams and picking out threads.

Selvage: A firmly woven strip formed along each lengthwise edge of the fabric.

Sewing in the groove or "stitching-in-the-ditch:" Attaching a binding so that no stitches show on the right side. The stitches are sunk into the groove or crease between the binding and the fabric being bound.

Shirt seam: So named because of its similarity to the double-stitched seams found on men's shirts. It is sometimes called a run-and-fell seam, dating from the days when these seams were sewn by hand.

Slipstitch: An almost invisible stitch formed by slipping the thread under a fold of fabric. It can be used to join two folded edges, or one folded edge to a flat surface.

Through and through or, through all layers: A machine stitch which goes through all the layers of fabric, as when sewing on a patch pocket or sewing the second row of stitching on a shirt seam.

Topstitch: Machine stitches done from the right side of a project for decorative and/or functional reasons.

Trim or clip corners: Cutting away excess fabric thus reducing bulk when points are turned right side out. Related variation: notching corners.

Trim seams: Cutting away some of the seam allowance, primarily to reduce bulk.

Tufting: Upholstery term used when fabric and padding are held firmly together at intervals, either with a tuft of threads, decorative ties, or buttons.

Wrong side: Wrong side is the side of the fabric that won't show once the project is completed.

Zigzag: Sewing machine function. Locking stitch with a side-to-side width as well as a stitch length. A zigzag stitch features more give than a straight stitch, making it less subject to breakage.

Patterns

Plastic Makeup Bag (page 34)

PHOTOCOPY AT 100%

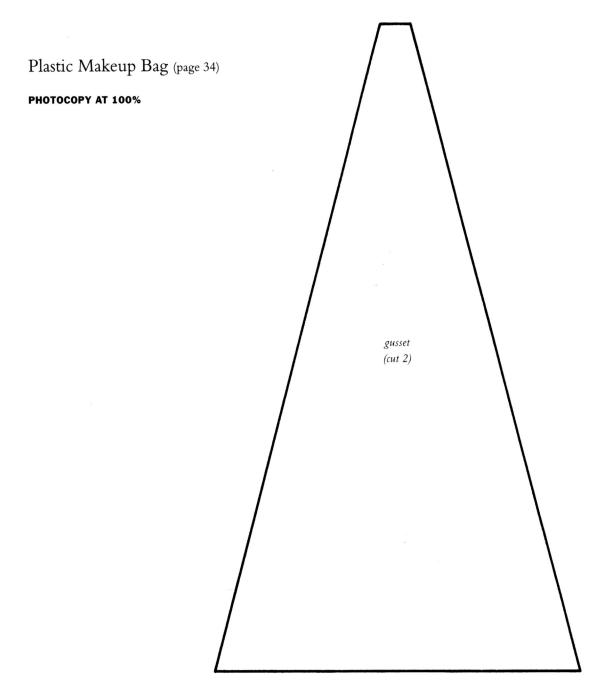

gusset
(cut 2)

Fabric-Covered Bath Tray (page 108) **PHOTOCOPY AT 400%**

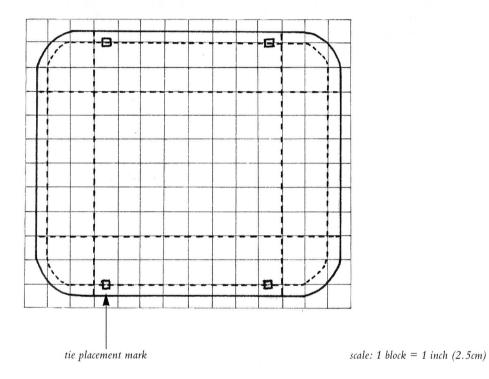

tie placement mark

scale: 1 block = 1 inch (2.5cm)

Sources

Contact each firm individually for an updated price list or catalog.

Atlanta Thread & Supply Company
695 Red Oak Road
Stockbridge, GA 30281
800-847-1001

Ballard Designs
1670 BeFoor Avenue NW
Atlanta, GA 30318-7528
800-367-2775 (orders) or
800-367-2810 (customer service)

Bed, Bath & Beyond
620 6th Avenue
New York, NY 10001
212-255-3550 or **800-462-3966**

Calico Corners
203 Gale Lane
Kennet Square, PA 19348-1764
800-213-6366

Chambers
Mail Order Dept.
P.O. Box 7841
San Francisco, CA 94120-7841
800-334-9790

Clotilde Inc.
Box 3000
Louisiana, MO 63353
800-772-2891

Coming Home
1 Lands' End Lane
Dodgeville, WI 53595-0001
800-345-3696

Crate & Barrel
P.O. Box 9059
Wheeling, IL 60090-9059
800-323-5461

Down Decor
Dept. SN, Box 4154
Cincinnati, OH 45204
800-792-3696

Gardeners Eden
P.O. Box 7307
San Francisco, CA 94120-7307
800-822-9600

Garnet Hill
Box 262, Main Street
Fraconia, NH 03580-0262
800-622-6216

Halcyon Yarn
12 School Street
Bath, ME 04530
800-341-0282

Herrschners Inc.
2800 Hoover Road
Stevens Point, WI 54492-0001
800-441-0838

Home-Sew
P.O. Box 4099
Bethlehem, PA 18018
610-867-3833

IKEA
IKEA Catalog Department
185 Discovery Drive
Colmar, PA 18915
800-434-4532

Keepsake Quilting
Route 25B
P.O. Box 1618
Centre Harbor, NH 03226-1618
800-865-9458

M&J Trimming
1008 6th Avenue
New York, NY 10018
212-391-6200

Nancy's Notions Ltd.
P.O. Box 683
Beaver Dam, WI 53916-0683
800-833-0690

Nasco Arts & Crafts
901 Janesville Avenue
P.O. Box 901
Fort Atkinson, WI 53538-0901
800-558-9595

Newark Dressmaker Supply
6473 Ruch Road
P.O. Box 20730
Lehigh Valley, PA 18002-0730
610-837-7500 or **800-736-6783**

Oppenheim's
P.O. Box 29
120 East Main Street
North Manchester, IN 46962-0052
800-461-6728

Oregon Tailor Supply Co., Inc.
2123 S.E. Division Street
P.O. Box 42284
Portland, OR 97242
800-678-2457

Pottery Barn
Mail Order Department
P.O. Box 7044
San Francisco, CA 94120-7044
800-922-5507

Sew/Fit Company
P.O. Box 397
Bedford Park, IL 60499
800-547-4739

Stretch & Sew Fabrics
8697 La Mesa Boulevard
La Mesa, CA 91941
619-589-8880

Sunrise Fabrics
264 West 40th Street
New York, NY 10018
212-768-7438

Thai Silks!
252 State Street
Los Altos, CA 94022
800-722-7455 or **800-221-7455 (CA)**

The Company Store
500 Park Plaza Drive
LaCrosse, WI 54601
800-285-3696

The Fabric Center
485 Electric Avenue
P.O. Box 8212
Fitchburg, MA 01420-8212
508-343-4402

Tinsel Trading Company
47 West 38th Street
New York, NY 10018
212-730-1030

Williams-Sonoma
Mail Order Department
P.O. Box 7456
San Francisco, CA 94120-7456
800-541-2233

Canadian Sources

The Cotton Patch
1717 Bedford Hwy
Bedford, NS B4W 1X3
902-861-2782

Bouclair
3149 Sources Bd.
Dollard-des-Ormeaux, QC H9B 1Z6
514-683-4711

La Maison de Calico
324 Lakeshore Blvd
Pointe Claire, QC H9S 4L7
514-695-0728

Omer DeSerres
334 Ste.-Catherine East
Montreal, QC H2X 1l7
800-363-0318 or **514-842-6637**

Rockland Textiles
2487 Kaladar Avenue
Ottawa, ON K1V 8B9
613-526-0333

Bouclair
1233 Donald Street
Ottawa, ON K1J 8W3
613-744-3982

Designer Fabric Outlet
1360 Queen St. W
Toronto, ON M6K 1L7
416-531-2810

The Fabric Cottage
16 Crowfoot Terrace NW
Calgary, AB T3G 4J8
403-241-3070

The Quilting Bee
1026 St. Mary's Rd
Winnipeg, MB R2M 3S6
204-254-7870

Homespun Craft Emporium
250A 2nd Avenue S
Saskatoon, SK S7K 1K9
306-652-3585

The Cloth Shop
4415 West 10th Avenue
Vancouver, BC V6R 2H8
604-224-1325

Metric Conversions

ENGLISH EQUIVALENTS

1/16in = 2mm	1/2in = 12mm or 1.2cm	1in = 2.5cm	1 qt = .95L
1/8in = 3mm	5/8in = 16mm or 1.6cm	2in = 5cm	1 pint = .47L
1/4in = 6mm	3/4in = 18mm or 1.8cm	3in = 7.5cm	1/2 cup = 120ml
3/16in = 5mm or 0.5cm	7/8in = 22mm or 2.2cm	4in = 10cm	1 cup = .24L
3/8in = 9.5mm or 0.9cm		5in = 12.5cm	3 lb = 1.36kg
		6in = 15cm	1 fluid oz = 30ml
		7in = 17.5cm	
		8in = 20.5cm	
		9in = 23cm	
		10in = 25.5cm	

English System to Metric

TO CHANGE:	INTO:	MULTIPLY BY:
Inches	Millimeters	25.4
Inches	Centimeters	2.54
Feet	Meters	0.305
Yards	Meters	0.914
Pints	Liters	.473
Quarts	Liters	.946
Gallons	Liters	3.78
Ounces	Grams	28.4
Pounds	Kilograms	.454

Metric to English System

TO CHANGE:	INTO:	MULTIPLY BY:
Millimeters	Inches	0.039
Centimeters	Inches	0.394
Meters	Feet	3.28
Meters	Yards	1.09
Liters	Pints	2.11
Liters	Quarts	1.06
Liters	Gallons	.264
Grams	Ounces	.035
Kilograms	Pounds	2.2

Credits

All color photography: Carl Tremblay

All styling: Ritch Holben

Patterns: (Pages 120-121) by Roberta Frauwirth.

Acknowledgments

A collection of this scope requires the talents of many people. Generous thanks to those at *Handcraft Illustrated* who assisted in its preparation: Art Director Elaine Hackney, Photographer Carl Tremblay, Stylist Ritch Holben, Editorial Assistant Melissa Nachatelo, Corporate Managing Editor Barbara Bourassa, and Publisher Christopher Kimball. Special thanks to John Kelsey for assistance editing the book; Elizabeth Cameron, Dawn Anderson, and Chippy Irvine for designing the many beautiful projects in this book; Ritch Holben for selecting many of the fabrics used in the projects; and Angela Miller and Coleen O'Shea of The Miller Agency for getting the Fast and Fabulous series off the ground.

About Handcraft Illustrated

Handcraft Illustrated is a sophisticated, yet accessible how-to magazine featuring craft and home decorating projects. Each 52-page quarterly issue includes approximately 40 different projects. The projects are accompanied by a full-color photograph, a complete materials list, precise step-by-step directions, and concise hand-drawn illustrations. All projects featured in the magazine are fully tested to ensure that the readers can make the designer-quality craft and home decorating projects at home.

Special departments include Quick Tips, an ongoing series of professional craft secrets, shortcuts, and techniques; Notes from Readers, providing detailed answers to readers' problems; Quick Home Accents, a unique pairing of materials and accessories designed to spur creative craft or decorating solutions; The Perfect Gift, offering creative solutions for designing, making, and packaging your own unique gifts; Quick Projects, a series of "theme-and-variation" projects featuring 4 to 6 versions of one beautiful but easy-to-make craft; and Sources and Resources, a retail and mail-order directory for locating materials and supplies used in the issue.

For a free trial issue of *Handcraft Illustrated*, phone 800-933-4447.

Index